Kiss My Fish
Tales of Chasing God Around the World

J. Bethany Anderson

Copyright © 2018 J. Bethany Anderson. All rights reserved.

ISBN: 978-1-9769-9266-7

Original cover art © 2018 by J. Bethany Anderson.
Cover art layout by Mark Fansler.

Unless otherwise noted, scripture quotations are from the *New International Version Bible* © 1973, 1978, 1984, 2011 by Biblica, Inc. Used by permission.
All rights reserved worldwide.

DEDICATION

To my grandmother and best friend, Dot,
who is now "running wild and free with Jesus"… and helping God find my husband.

TABLE OF CONT(IN)ENTS

TABLE OF CONT(IN)ENTS vi

FULL SPEED AHEAD ix
    Pre-Ramblings 11

HOME SOIL: USA 15
    Hello, Goodbye 17
    Knobby-Kneed Me 23
    Moon Walk 27
    Monkey Chaos 31
    Whoopee Cushions & Candy Cigarettes 35
    Happy Family 39
    Heartstrings & Pie 43
    The Day of Whales 49
    Collecting Stories 55
    Kiss My Fish 60

GONE EAST: France, Switzerland, The United Kingdom, & The Netherlands 66
    To Be Known 67
    Paradigm Shift 70
    Swiss Cheese & Living Water 75
    Mountain Girl 81
    The Wildness of Aliveness 87
    Frozen Exasperation 95
    Jump 103
    Lingering Presence 109
    The Hands of God 114
    The Kiss of Alan 120
    Don't Watch Your Step 123

DOWN UNDER: South Africa & Australia 126
    Voices 127
    Expectancy is Abstract Art 135
    Leo-'ello 141

Yellow Joy 147
From Under the Veil of Chaos 151
Four Postcards 157
You Are Beautiful 161
Hummingbirds & Kittens 164
More Than a Haircut 168
Paint with God 175

WHEREVER… We'll Go **179**
Post-Ramblings 180

ACKNOWLEDGMENTS **182**

ABOUT THE AUTHOR **185**

FULL SPEED AHEAD

Pre-Ramblings

"When shall we live, if not now?" ~ *Seneca*

Once I roller-skated over my wrist. I realize that sounds impossible, but for my twig-armed, seven-year old, roller-skating pretzel self, I had it coming. I was showing-off for my friends as their parents were shuffling them out of my driveway, and my zeal overtook my common sense. I tucked into a ball to speed down my driveway hill, and, at the same time turned my head around to wave charismatically at my adoring fans. When I turned back around to give myself a boost of speed, I miscalculated the exact position of where my pushing hand should touch ground, and then it was too late. With a *bump bump*, I roller-skated over my wrist. As you might imagine, my body continued forward and my arm remained stationary behind me, until I forcefully yanked it to join the rest of my little body.

I have been traveling full-speed ahead since I was a child. I still turn my head, wooed by the ones I love and by the ones I meet by God's design around the globe, but I also try to keep my eyes fixed ahead on Jesus, because I believe chasing the God of adventure is worth it.

I love metaphors. They make me tick. My friends know this, and many have plastered me with word pictures that describe my life.

Mary Poppins. One of my mentors says I pop in with the east wind, splatter some life, color, music and joy around, then I'm out with the same wind that brought me in.

Maria from the Sound of Music. My dad looks at me teasingly with a glimmer in his eye and says, "How *do* you catch a cloud and pin her down, Maria?"

A whirlwind. I was recently lunching with some ladies from my Bible Study group. After my discourse on a job search that could land me in yet another city, one friend looked at me and mentioned that I'm like a whirlwind. She said I came into the group with warmth, encouragement, and a zest for life, and that now maybe it's time for me to travel down the road to the next place to bless others.

A beach ball. In November of 2008, when I was living in South Africa, a friend of mine said she was praying for me and saw that I was like a colorful beach ball on a crowded beach bouncing from people group to people group. Everyone enjoyed the ball, laughing and celebrating, as it bounced from one group to another. With that image, she spoke Zephaniah 3:9 over me:

> *"I will purify the lips of the peoples, that all of them may call on the name of the Lord and serve him shoulder to shoulder."*

It's currently 2017, nine years later, and these images – *Mary Poppins, Maria, a whirlwind, a beach ball* - couldn't ring more true in predicting the pattern and joy of my life – traveling from city to city, country to country, planting my roots long enough to connect deeply with and love people before uprooting to move along to the next place and the next God-adventure.

I am *Mary Poppins*.

I am *Maria*.

I am a *whirlwind*.

I am a *beach ball*.

I am a nomad, traveling full-speed ahead, chasing after the God of love, life, and adventure.

Our culture sometimes has negative connotations of such a lifestyle. In fact, the mindset that says you have to stay in one place, rooted and grounded, to be effective, is one that I've had to battle my whole life. I don't believe it is everyone's calling to bounce around like a beach ball, infecting the world with enthusiasm, silliness, and a passion for the gospel, but it is mine.

With that backdrop, the stories on the following pages have come to be. Some of the stories are about friends I've met along the way or family members that are near and dear to me. Others are simply about me. One thing is certain though, God, the Great Weaver Himself, has woven them all.

I'm a journal junkie. I journal *everything*. I use my journal to take sermons notes, record revelations, thoughts, prophetic dreams and poignant conversations. In fact, the stories on the following pages are in thanks to the thousands and thousands of words on pages from my past. I am thankful for the ink that spills from my heart out of my pen onto clean, white pages. I am thankful because with every word, every sentence, every point of punctuation, I am reminded of God's story in my story. I am reminded of His story in you, too.

I am reminded of His promises, His words and His faithfulness. I am reminded that though I often travel alone, I am never alone. I am reminded that He never leaves me, never forsakes me, never abandons me, never leaves me hanging, or never turns His back on me. He is always there. And on the days when I think He's not near, I open any one of my journals, and He jumps off the pages, shouting, "I was there then and I am here now."

The following collection of stories speaks to following God into the unknown adventures of life. As soon as I think I know what's next, God always surprises me with a new journey to embark upon. He keeps me on my toes, not just so I can have flexible feet, but also so that He can take my flexibility and use it for His glory. My wandering feet are a mosaic testimony to His goodness, faithfulness, provision, leading, grace, love and mercy in my life.

I consider it an honor and a privilege to walk this path with Him, *for* Him.

When we surrender to Him, leaving our wayward worldly desires behind, we are set free for the greatest adventure of all: following Him whole-heartedly into a life of color, adventure and abundance.

I'm thankful, oh so thankful. At the end of the day, this adventure with God ignites this praise of my heart: WITH HIM, IT'S ALL WORTH IT.

These stories give bones to that praise, "It's all worth it!" I invite you to follow my cultural journey as I jump from continent to continent, making my home in six countries over a period of ten years. I invite you to glean insight from my parallel journey of faith as I travel on overseas adventures pursuing God into unknown places, wrestling through dry seasons and rejoicing in high ones, Join me as I surrender parts of myself along the way, navigate the ups and downs of relationships, and negotiate seasons of transition with the "hellos" and "goodbyes" and all the emotions that come with that. I've put my heart on the following pages in the hopes that you will engage with God on a new level.

Once you close this book and walk away, I pray that you will be emboldened with a new courage to keep walking and keep pressing on. I pray that you will know that, at the end of the day, this beautiful, colorful, and unpredictable adventure with God is *all worth it*. My prayer is that you will discover the same faithfulness of God in your own life, as you chase after Him, allowing Him to lead you on your own faith adventures.

Come, let's chase the God of love, life, and adventure together and see where He takes us and what He does…

J. Bethany Anderson

HOME SOIL: USA

CHAPTER 1

Hello, Goodbye

"Man cannot discover new oceans unless he has the courage to lose sight of the shore." ~ André Gide

I grew up in a world of color and laughter, a world where life revolved around family vacations, school plays, ballet and gymnastics, art and stories, homemade movies, close childhood friends, amateur improv performances, imaginatively themed birthday parties, church activities, and Jesus.

I was a happy, bubbly, outgoing child. In fact, the way in which I was born seemed to dictate those characteristics of my personality. I entered the world "sunny-side up," smiling and glowing with platinum blonde hair, so much so that my mother freaked out when the nurse announced, "Ooh, she has platinum hair!" because she thought something was terribly wrong.

I have my parents to thank for the atmosphere of fun that pervaded my childhood. On many occasions, I would scuffle down the stairs sleepy-eyed to find my mother dancing in the kitchen, all while crafting the most amazing animal-shaped pancakes. I used to play this game where I'd time myself to see how quickly I could suck-up the chocolate chip eyes like a vacuum cleaner sucks up dirt. It was extremely lady-like.

If it wasn't my mom that entertained my mornings, it was my dad. It was his job every Sunday to wake my two brothers and me up for church. This was no ordinary task. My dad outworked this job with enthusiasm and excellence, oftentimes slapping a bow on his baldhead, and then creating a ruckus by jumping up, clapping, and chanting through my cheerleading megaphone, "Get out of bed, sleepy-heads! Two bits, four bits, six bits a dollar, out of the bed, stand up and holler!" I gained my non-morning person reputation from these very moments, and though I would snap at my dad to "Leave me alone," I was secretly giggling in delight underneath my covers.

My childhood was built on a strong foundation of fun and laughter. My younger brother, Casey, received the full brunt of this growing up. When he was a baby, it was my older brother's and my job to keep him smiling, no matter what. He would start whimpering about something, and Zak and I would step in and make a goofy face, or tickle him into laughing oblivion. And that's the way that we dealt with most conflict in our family – *"If you can get 'em laughing, you've got 'em."*

Many years later, while working as an au pair in France, I had a revelation. I was taking care of two young Cambodian girls, aged six and seven. One particular evening, the youngest girl refused to take her evening bath. So rather than fighting with her, I picked her up and put her in the bathtub next to her sister. She did not like this, and jumped out of the tub with vengeance in her eyes. She punched me while screaming, "I hate you! Go home!"

After a few minutes of this ridiculously dramatic tantrum, I just laughed to myself. After that episode, which eventually was dissipated by the waters of a warm, bubbly bath, I phoned my mom, asking the all-important question, "Did I ever behave that way as a child?" Her reply of "No way, we would've just laughed at you" wrapped-up my childhood in one word. *Humor.* It was the solution for most things.

In fact, I blame that word for establishing my daily silliness quotient. Humor is key. It is foundational. And it continues to be part of my everyday life. In fact even now as an adult, when I'm having a down day, my mom will dress in a big smile and say, "Remember Bethany, be joyful."

Apart from perhaps the abnormal dose of humor, I had a pretty normal upbringing. I was a ballerina. I was an ice skater. I was a painter. I was a gymnast. I was a poet. I was a cheerleader. I was a roller-skater. I was an actress. I was a puppeteer. I'm sorry. Did I say normal?

I guess it wasn't super normal after all. *But then again, what is, really?*

I remember being a child and thinking that I was different from my friends. I never really understood why, because on the outside, everything seemed pretty much the same as everyone around me, other than my array of bizarre outfits I assembled for school on a near daily basis.

When I was at the end of my eighth grade year, I wore one of my favorite outfits on the day we got to visit the high school for our freshman cheerleader induction. I wore Beetle-Juice black and white tights, dark mid-calf combat boots, a black short-sleeve shirt, and denim shorts overalls. I got some stares from my fellow squad members, but the Varsity cheerleaders complimented me on my "creativity and confidence."

Besides my leanings towards "interesting" fashion, I knew from a very young age that there was a unique path set out in front of me for my life. I knew that my life was never really going to look like everyone else's.

My parents traveled quite a bit because my dad and grandfather ran an international business. I remember my "goodbye ritual" with my dad when he would get ready to leave for another international jaunt. I would wait in my bedroom until my dad came into the room to say goodbye. Then I would pop-up like a sizzling popcorn kernel and clasp my boney little fingers around my dad's neck. I would say, "Dad, I'm a giant necklace! You have to wear me and take me with you!" My threats didn't ever last too long because eventually my fingers would slide down his neck, and I would dramatically collapse on my bed. And then I knew then that I really had to say goodbye. Though I would try to prolong this "hugging game" as much as possible, my dad would eventually woo me to sleep, promising me goodies and stories of adventure upon his return.

And that's where it all started for me, in regards to two major things in my life. First, with every exotic trip my dad took, I went with him. My little girl imagination dreamed that I was seeing all these new and exciting things, and I had the international doll collection to prove that I had been places. My bedroom shelves were lined with tokens from China to Nigeria, Egypt to England, Switzerland to Australia, and Saudi Arabia to Brazil. I couldn't remember half the names of my dolls because I couldn't even pronounce them! Watching my dad travel the world taught me to crave "going," even if just in my imagination at the time. Secondly, I learned to despise goodbyes.

As a little girl, I invented the "necklace game," because as long as I could keep my dad in front of me, it meant that I didn't have to say goodbye. It meant I could keep him with me in my room. But it never failed that when I dropped from his neck and crashed to my bed, it signaled the moment I dreaded the most – the moment of "goodbye."

Years and a plethora of countries later, with countless friends scattered across the globe, this is still the one word I despise more than anything else in the English language: *goodbye*. Actually, I really hate the word moist, too, for other reasons.

I usually describe myself to people as a "Jack(ie) of all trades." I have more interests and passions than I can keep up with, and a mind that is constantly racing, keeping me volleying between this task or that passion. I'm not a person who excels amazingly at *one* thing, but one who is mediocre at lots of things. Someone called me a Renaissance Lady recently. I'll take it, as long as I can change out my wardrobe and wash my hair regularly.

One thing I do have expertise in, though, is saying goodbye. I don't like this about myself. I wish I was a professional surfer or that I excelled at building birdhouses or something. I don't. I am experienced in the way of goodbyes. It comes with the territory of being a global citizen, and in my case, a person who travels more than they cook.

I'm a closure person. I don't just want it. I *need* it. When I'm texting with a friend, I want to be the one who sends the final text in that thread. When I'm watching a sitcom and someone exits the room leaving the door open, it drives me crazy! I cannot handle it. I want to reach through the TV and slam the door shut.

I have this strange closure habit. When I'm getting ready to move away from a place, I become really present with people where I am. I realize that we should always be present with others, but this is highlighted as one of my top priorities when I'm about to change my geography.

For example, when I was living in Switzerland, I would typically call my parents every Sunday night. When I was preparing to move, though, I told them I wouldn't call them for my final weeks in Europe because I wanted to focus my time and energy there. In my mind I was thinking, *I'm about to be back in Texas with my family and have to leave my friends here, so I'm going to spend every waking moment with the people here that I won't see when I move back to Texas.* Makes sense, right?

Goodbyes mean leaving people, and I hate that. I can't even handle leaving a party early, let alone leaving people halfway around the world that I love, especially when I have no idea if, when, or where I'll see them again. Even now, the thought of the well-worn road of goodbyes is paved with faces that prick my heart with sadness, though blanketed by thankfulness for the intersection of our lives. I think of Carmen, Matt, and Cat in Australia, Linda and Cornel in South Africa, Kerstin, Hannah, Petrova, Anto, Emma, Natalie, and Caroline in England, Paul and Becky, Craig and Sharon, and Ian in Switzerland.

I could go on and on because I am a people-person to my own detriment. I live and breathe by relationships and connectedness. When I feel disconnected, it's like my world is literally caving-in. I don't handle goodbyes well, and I've definitely never done breakups well.

In fact, I believe God has protected me from a string of broken romantic relationships because He knows exactly how He created me – as a person who needs closure and as one who cannot cope with severed relationships on any level.

I despise goodbyes. I really do.

But here's the thing: I've learned that chasing after the God of adventure means that goodbyes come with the lifestyle. Saying "yes" to God sometimes means saying "no" to something or someone else. That's hard and oftentimes painful, but it is always worth it.

If I had never had the courage to leave Texas that first time back in 2003, my life wouldn't be filled by the richness of deep friendships I have with people all over the globe. Sometimes it takes leaving to gain more than you ever thought possible.

One of my favorite quotes by André Gide says, "Man cannot discover new oceans unless he has the courage to lose sight of the shore."

It's true. Letting go, leaving, moving on, saying goodbye. All of these things can be painful, but we never know what we are missing – what God has in store for us and others – when we grasp so tightly to the things we know and love with an unwillingness to let go. .

Leo, a dear South African friend of mine, always prayed with his palms open. When I asked him why he did this, he told me, "Bethany, you can't receive from God when your hands are already closed."

I love this picture. I can't receive the fullness of what God has to offer for my life and the lives of others until I have the courage to say goodbye when He's asking me to do so. I can fight it, avoid it, clench my fists, and close my palms, but I will miss out on the adventure of life and love that He has before me.

I still hate goodbyes, but here's my resolve. I will say hello to goodbyes for the sake of God, and for the sake of the richness that I will behold on the other side when He connects me to people in that place. I will say hello to goodbyes because sometimes it is in saying goodbye to one thing, person, or job that you find yourself in the center of God's will - a place where you can run freely into all that He has for you with open hands.

"Hello, goodbye."

CHAPTER 2

Knobby-Kneed Me

"God doesn't want something from us, He simply wants us." ~ C.S. Lewis

As a seven-year-old knobby-kneed little girl, I waited the whole year for the opportunity to shine in the limelight at the Burks Elementary School Talent Show. In fact, in order to practice for my on-stage appearance, I would dress in my mother's finest colored hosiery socks, layering eight or so colors atop one another in memorable 80s fashion, and slather thick red lipstick on my non-existent lips. Then I'd throw on a lagoon-blue sweatshirt, stuffed with a pillow to enhance my sinewy figure. I would prance around and shimmy on the bed in front of her humongous mirror, contorting my face into "looks" in order to achieve the best potential crowd reaction. I did this on a regular basis, and if I wasn't in a costume frolicking on my mother's bed, I was mimicking the girl in the Kraft cheese commercials in a hallway mirror.

One particular year, the mothers of my girls' Bluebird Troop arranged for us to perform a little sketch to the song, *My Special Date, Dad!* The plan was for us to sing, dance, get ready, and be picked-up by our dads for our special date, all while onstage in front of the audience.

In rehearsals before the show, I perfected my moves and "getting ready" techniques in order to shine like a superstar on the big day. Though I already stuck out because my hair was like curly-Q-ed yellow straw, over-fried by perms, I was also a stellar little dancer. So this show was going to be as simple as *1-2-3*.

When the big evening came, the music started and out we bopped onstage, while our dads watched and waited in the wings. We swayed, blew kisses, and winked at the audience, all while dancing and singing to the familiar song:

> *I've got a date tonight at eight*
> *I want to look my best*
> *I'll wear my pearls and comb my curls*
> *And wear my party dress*
> *My makeup will look snazzy with powder on my nose*
> *And boy will I look jazzy in shoes with pointed toes*
> *The time is near when he'll appear and I can hardly wait*
> *He'll say "hello" and off we'll go. I'm going on a date!*

After wooing the audience for a bit, the musical interlude started and we stepped back to our dressing tables to unroll our curlers, put on our lipstick, and de-robe ourselves to reveal our lovely dresses underneath. We had sixty seconds to primp and be back to the front of the stage to finish our dance steps. For the *grand finale*, our daddy dates were going to walk onstage and escort us off hand-in-hand.

I couldn't wait to see my dad's big smile. I knew he'd be so proud of me. I was ready to strut my stuff with my him right beside me.

The problem was my stuff wouldn't come off!

During the sixty-second musical interlude, I had stepped back, just like the other six girls, to primp and change out of my robe. My nervous fingers fumbled to untie my robe, but I couldn't get it untangled.

Apparently during the rehearsal, I became fidgety with nerves and tied my robe into a death-knot. My clammy little fingers couldn't get the cotton strings out of their pink-plaid knot bond. I pulled and I struggled, and even resorted to violently grabbing my innocent friend by her curls and demanding her assistance with a facial expression that screamed, "This is my moment to shine! Help me!"

The helpless look on her face told me that she was going to focus on her own limelight. She had a show to perform, after all. So there I was, all alone in my crisis, while stuck at the back of the stage panicking like a lost child at the State Fair of Texas.

After it struck me that my plans for positive limelight had failed miserably, I immediately lost any semblance of control like a mini-diva gone mad, and belted out a loud *hmmmmph* as tears electrified the blue in my big eyes and heated my face. I thought I was alone in my temper tantrum until I heard bursts of laughter in the wings and from the far corners of the entire room. My outburst had drawn the attention of the whole audience when my twig arms had flown up in Bette-Middler-style to paint drama in the sky.

To my dismay, my fellow dancers were now already back at the front of the stage looking all pretty and perfect, singing:

I had a time! A real good time! The best I've every had!
'Cause he's my guy, I'll tell you why - My date tonight is DAD!

I was standing alone at the back, the volume of my sobbing escalating quickly.

And then something magical happened. I heard my dad's voice above all the chaos in my heart and mind. I heard him above the music and above the tap-dancing of my friends. I heard him above the sharp laughter of the audience, and above the murmurs of other fathers in the wings.

I heard him loudly and clearly encouraging me, "Bethany, I'm right here! Come to me."

I immediately did an about-face and sprinted offstage into the arms of my daddy, waiting in the wings for his little diva. He picked me up and hugged me, assuring me that everything was going to be okay. And it was.

I'm thankful for a father who has painted such an incredible picture of the fatherhood of God for me.

I'm thankful that in moments where chaos rules my heart and mind, in moments where the music and the noise of life is too loud, in moments where sharp laughter or judgment or criticism from others is overwhelming, I'm thankful that God's voice rings out, "Bethany, I'm right here! Come to me."

I'm thankful He is always waiting in the wings, beaming his big dad smile and waiting for me to come running into His arms. His encouragement, His embrace is everything.

That day at the Burks Talent Show, my dad told me something else. He said, "I'm proud of you, not because you're an excellent performer, but I'm proud of who you are and always will be."

When I run into the arms of God, I remember that it doesn't matter what I do for Him. He doesn't care how many books I write, or how many songs I perform, how successful I am financially, or how spiritually stable I am. He sees me for me. He loves me because He created me. And He is proud of me for just being me.

He doesn't want my performance. He just wants me. Plain and simple, knobby-kneed me.

CHAPTER 3

Moon Walk

"As people are walking all the time, in the same spot, a path appears."
~ John Locke

I've always blamed my older brother for my passionate dislike of country music. You would, too, if you had to ride with him to school everyday in his muffler-less deafening pickup truck, all while he blared the likes of Toby Keith and Pat Green into your bleeding ears. Besides, I was in the fragile adolescent stage of my teenage years.

One particular morning of my freshman year, I arrived at school late and disconcerted, my thoughts trying to rebuke the mantra that had just been sung over my life, *I'm the queen of my doublewide trailer.* It was a typical day, but atypically windy outside. My brother had it easy. He could sneak into his theater class because he entered the school through a backdoor. I, on the other hand, had to pass the assistant principal every time I was late.

The routine went something like this:

Mr. Assistant Principal, with a fiery nod of disapproval, "Anderson! Late again?"

Me, innocently batting my eyes, "I'm sorry. It's my brother's fault!"

This was our daily exchange, just not *this* particular morning

I walked in late, and thought I would receive the normal greeting. The tone was very different, though, "Anderson!?!?" It was inflected with high tones, communicating a shocked question, rather than a routine reprimand. Mr. Assistant Principal stared at me with a look of disapproval and then remained silent. I sheepishly said my normal, "Sorry, it's my brother's fault," and kept walking. (Little did I know what that actually meant to him that day!)

I grew more and more unsettled by the odd question and the bizarre look on his face as I traveled across the campus towards the open corridor and staircase.

After rounding the corner, I headed up the first flight of stairs, but experienced a strange feeling. It was unnaturally breezy on my backside. Simultaneous to this feeling, I heard a company of voices laughing in hearty unison behind me. My instinct shouted to my hands, *Do a wardrobe check!* I frantically fumbled my fingers behind me to reach for my skirt. And then, mid-step, I froze. My skirt had gone A.W.O.L. No skirt, nada, nothing - only cotton-panty-covered butt cheeks.

After what felt like ten minutes of searching, I finally realized to my shock and horror that my skirt had jumped up my back and gotten tangled under my backpack straps. The audacity of those stinkin' gale-force winds outside had played a nasty trick on me! Much to my humiliation, I had an audience of teenage boys snickering and following my moon like it was the moon in the night sky.

I may not be fond of country music, but I am fond of Michael Jackson. I became a pro at doing the *Moon Walk* that day.

In fact, I just kept walking. I walked and walked until I reached my destination, my classroom. I didn't let a little embarrassing inconvenience stop me that day. I didn't sit in a corner and cry. I didn't run to the bathroom and hide. I didn't call my mom and ask her to pick me up from school. I didn't dig a hole and crawl into it forever. I didn't panic. I didn't freeze permanently.

I toughed it out, laughed it off, and kept walking to class.

One of the most important lessons I've learned in life is to just keep walking.

When days are hard, when things don't go as planned, when life feels drab or overwhelming or too painful, just keep walking.

When you're crying in your cereal, or bawling as you drive down the road, when you're upset at a coworker, or heartbroken from a severed relationship, just keep walking.

When you've just been given the news that you or someone you love has cancer, when you've just lost your job, when you have to uproot your family for your spouse's job, just keep walking.

I recognize that it is hard to keep walking. I often find myself over thinking everything. I overanalyze this, pick that apart, I dissect what he said, what she did, or what that situation means. My cousin, Rebecca, laughingly reminds me that we both struggle with a disease called, "analysis paralysis." We joke about it, but on the flip side, it's a very serious disease of *self.* It has literally stopped me in my tracks at times. It has arrested me from making big decisions. It has delayed important conversations. And though I am a huge believer that God's timing is perfect, I also believe that we can impede His timing by our inability to act and step out in faith when He calls and directs. When we stop walking, our *walk with Him* is halted, our dreams are put on hold, and we are paralyzed in the in-between.

I have just come out of a season of life where I *stopped walking* for too long. I allowed the waves to crash over me and spin me in circles. I allowed the rough waters to throw me completely off-course. Every single aspect of my life was paralyzing. My over thinking everything didn't help me, either. It kept me frozen in place.

I recently quit a job, which from the outside, looked like a perfect fit for me. But here's what I know to be true: For two and a half years, I wrestled internally about everything that this job represented for me. The hardest part is that it was a job in ministry. Of course, it was where I was "supposed to be." But it was eating away at my soul, because it was symbolic of the fact that I had *stopped walking.*

I believe in God's Sovereignty, that He uses all things for His good like <u>Romans 8:28</u> says: *"And we know that in all things God works for the good of those who love him, who have been called according to his purpose."*

I also know that He redeems all things and is making things new like <u>Isaiah 43:19</u> says, *"See, I am doing a new thing! Now it springs up; do you not perceive it? I am making a way in the wilderness and streams in the wasteland."*

I understand all of this because God is a good God, but I also know He calls us to just *keep walking.* When the seasons are tough, when the storm is raging. Don't stop. Don't freeze. Don't get caught up in "analysis paralysis" of life, allowing that to rob you of all the gifts and blessings in front of you. Just keep walking. Trust and fix your eyes on Jesus.

I am reminded of the story of Peter in Matthew 14, where he *chose* to get out of the boat. Before he chose to walk towards Jesus, though, he made a remarkable statement directed towards the ghostly figure walking on the sea, *"Lord, if it is you, command me to come to you on the water."* (Matthew 14:28)

I am struck by Peter's forwardness and ask myself, "Why would he *initiate* this step of faith?" Perhaps it's because He sees Jesus' words just before as an invitation, *"Take heart; it is I. Do no be afraid."* (Matthew 14:27) Perhaps it's because everything in him wanted it to be Jesus, so that he could jump out of the boat to be with Him.

Whatever the case, I find myself wondering about the times I wish I could just jump out of the boat to walk on water towards Jesus, but feel paralyzed because the risk seems too great. That is where my over-analytical side becomes the disease of *self*, the disease that robs me of the joy of risking *all* to be with Jesus. Because wherever Jesus is, the risk is worth it to get there.

If it means walking forward through the storm, if it means walking on waves in raging seas, if it means walking away from someone or something, I choose to keep walking. I choose to keep walking, because just as Peter did, I want to walk straight to the source of my faith. In my moments of fear, doubt, uncertainty, unworthiness, emptiness, and brokenness, I want to walk with Jesus. To do so, I have to walk *to* Him first. I just have to keep walking. I encourage you to do the same.

Pick up your feet, put a smile on your face, and let the laughter of those teenage boys in the hallway become your soundtrack as you just keep doing the *Moon Walk*.

CHAPTER 4

Monkey Chaos

"I'm letting you know what I need, calling out for help and lifting my arms toward your inner sanctum." ~ Psalm 28:2 (MSG)

Most summers my family would sneak away from our Texas routine and take an adventure to some exciting place like Florida, Hawaii, or California. When my parents surveyed us kids as to what type of destination we'd like to visit, we always yelled in unison, "The beach!" My parents only asked us because they knew this is exactly what we'd say, and they always wanted to visit the beach, too.

In the summer of 1987, when I was seven years old, my family adventured beyond the United States and flew to Cozumel, Mexico. We did our vacation usual – building sandcastles on the beach, bodysurfing the clear blue waters, sunning our pasty skin into a bronze glow, and splashing in the resort pool for hours upon hours. After several days of these activities, my parents wanted to change our scenery, so we rented a Jeep Wrangler to explore the island back roads.

Our exploration led us to a secluded spot at the edge of the island called the Naked Turtle Beach, which boasted only of a small cantina and the most amazing oceanfront climbing-boulders a child could ever imagine. After running like crabs in and out of the ocean spray and repeatedly scaling those boulders, my brothers and I decided to visit the cantina for a refreshing Coke to cool us off.

When we walked inside, there was a surprise waiting for us!

I am an animal lover. I love all kinds of animals, but that day, standing before me, was my favorite animal - the cutest, most-squeezable, little monkey.

He was standing guard near the bar and attached to a long chain. With a bounce in my step, I glanced at my mom, seeking the go-ahead to pet my newfound friend. She nodded in approval and pulled out her camera. In my very fashionable 1980s hot pink bikini and white laceless Keds, I waltzed over to the monkey, bent down to his level and began to pat his little monkey head, saying, "Hello monkey. You're so cute." In what I now understand to be patronizing monkey behavior, he returned the sentiment and started patting *my* head.

And then, unpredictable chaos ensued.

The monkey had spotted my perfectly positioned pigtails, one shooting off of either side of my very blonde head. His boney little monkey fingers grabbed one in each hand and started steering his fake car with my head acting as the steering wheel. He made this wild *ooohh ooohh eee eee ahh ahh* sound, all while aggressively forcing my head in a left-to-right repeated motion. I don't know where he thought he was driving us, all I know is that what started out as this thrilling surprise, quickly escalated into violence. My head was being thrown back and forth, to and fro, and my vision was blurry. All I could see was this demon monkey finding pure joy in my pain and confusion. Tears began to stream from my hot face because his conniving little fingers were ripping out my hair, and all the movement was giving me a pounding headache.

In that moment, all I could think was, *Help! This isn't fun anymore! This monkey is hurting me! Mom! Dad! Someone, rescue me!*

In that moment, fear paralyzed me. Things quickly went from fun, laughter, and a monkey friend to torment, fear and a monkey nemesis

After several photographs of this unbelievable scene unfolding before my family's eyes, and just as I was at my wit's end with the monkey and his attempts to pull my hair out of my head, my dad stepped in and loosened the grip of those sticky monkey fingers on my pigtails. Ever so gently, my dad took my hand in his and pulled me away from the little terror. After my tears stopped flowing and I caught my breath, I knew everything would be all right.

Even though I was in the middle of a terrifying and unpredictable situation for a child, not knowing how things would end with the crazy monkey, I actually *knew* that my dad was never just going to stand there and watch me struggle. I knew that he wasn't going to let anything happen to me. Those sticky monkey fingers wouldn't hold me captive forever.

In my experience, God is exactly like that. He never abandons us to fend for ourselves. He doesn't leave us in the middle of unpredictable chaos forever. He is in control, and all He has to do is step in and loosen the monkey grip. Those fingers won't hold us captive forever.

I'm utterly thankful for that aspect of God, because I don't know about you, but I often find myself in seasons of life that feel completely out of control, unmanageable, or unpredictable. Things aren't right. They're not easy. My life isn't panning out how I planned. That person wasn't supposed to die. That relationship wasn't supposed to end. That job was supposed to be mine. She wasn't supposed to be there. I was. He wasn't supposed to do that. I was. Life wasn't supposed to be like this. It was supposed to look a lot better.

The list goes on and on, and if I allow myself to dwell on the pandemonium that life sometimes brings, I get overwhelmed. Peace exits, and panic enters.

But I stop. I sit still. I reflect on God because He *is* in control.

Proverbs 16:9 says, *"The heart of man plans his way, but the Lord establishes his steps."* I am so thankful that He is in control and that I am not. I am thankful that when life seems chaotic, He steps in, loosens those sticky monkey fingers and takes my hand in His and pulls me away from the chaos and into Himself.

What's funny about my monkey "friend" from 1987 is that my dad's secretary visited the same beach cantina years later. She found the monkey stuffed and mounted on the wall, and even brought us a picture to prove it.

God doesn't just give us peace. He doesn't just rescue us in the moment. He even goes as far to stuff the monkey and mount it on the wall as a reminder that in His timing, all seasons of chaos come to an end. They won't hold us captive forever.

My prayer is that we have eyes to see the light on the other side – the rescue, the freedom, the joy – it's coming. Hold on, wait it out. God is going to extend His hand to us, and pull us into His safe.

Presence, out of the chaos that captivates our hearts and minds, actions and beliefs.

Until then, though, keep your pigtails away from crazy monkeys in cantinas.

Chapter 5

Whoopee Cushions & Candy Cigarettes

*"He drew a circle that shut me out - Heretic, rebel, a thing to flout.
But love and I had the wit to win: We drew a circle and took him in!"
~ Edwin Markham, from the poem," Outwitted"*

There's something in our broken humanity that causes us to rebel. Perhaps it's the thrill of trying not to get caught. Perhaps it's just fun to break out of the mold of "good behavior" at times. Perhaps it is that we are creatures drawn to sin and rebellion because that's our nature.

My cousin, Rebecca, and I were perfect little angels, and every summer we went to spend a week with our Aunt Sally in Houston.

We had several traditions when we visited, such as: going to the water park, shopping sprees at the Galleria, riding in my uncle's shop van at high speeds on the bumpiest road in Houston, renting movies, and eating lunches with my aunt's highfalutin friends. Well, one summer when we were nine years old, my aunt invited my baby cousin, Laura, Rebecca's little sister, to kill our week of bliss.

This disturbing news caused our evil twins to hijack our angelic personalities that summer week.

One incident in particular stands out. We went to the Galleria, and my aunt gave us money and the freedom to spend it as we pleased. With fire in our eyes, we headed straight to the gag store and bought a packet of candy cigarettes, a Whoopee Cushion, and a can of aromatic prank spray.

We met back up with my aunt shortly after our shopping spree, stashing all of our purchased goods in my oversized preteen purse, and headed to lunch at Chili's with my aunt's friend. We had chips and salsa, and pleasant conversation until suddenly, there was a scream from our new friend at the table, "Ooooh! What was that cold thing on my leg?"

My aunt looked to her friend's leg and replied, "Are you okay? What are you talking about?"

My aunt's friend continued, "Something cold hit my leg. It felt like hairspray. And did you hear that noise? I'm sure someone passed gas!"

My aunt, scanning the room curiously and pinching her nostrils now, said, "Ohhh... and *what* is that horrid smell?"

In a moment, their innocent curiosity faded and revelation struck like lightning. My aunt whipped her head in our direction and spewed *The Inquisition*, "Bethany! Rebecca! What have you done?"

Sheepishly, we giggled, thinking, as the angels we normally were, that it might be our last moment here on earth and that our sweet laughter might be our only hope of escaping alive.

It didn't work.

Oh. Crap.

That's exactly what we had done.

Rebecca and I had staged a *potty humor* prank that had drastically failed! While my aunt and her friend were talking boring national politics, I had sneakily pulled the spray out of my bag, and pressed my mischievous finger to the nozzle. Unfortunately my aim was terribly off, because though I intended to just mist the air, I doused my aunt's friend's caramel colored pantyhose instead. The culprit was the most vile smelling fart spray, and there was now a visibly wet fart-spray-circle on her left calf.

To make matters worse, Rebecca perfectly timed the *sound* that was distinctly heard by my aunt's friend. She sat on the Whoopee Cushion at the exact moment the spray escaped its can.

Crap again.

We got in so much trouble with my aunt that we were sent outside, where we sat defeated on the curb, feeling a weight of shame and guilt, while pretending to smoke our candy cigarettes.

Reflecting back on this rebellious incident with my cousin, I can't help but wonder where Jesus would be in this story.

Would he be pointing His finger and reprimanding us for our behavior? Perhaps. Would He be mad at us for embarrassing Him? Perhaps. Would He send us outside to think about our actions? Perhaps. Would He be right in doing all of this? I think so.

But I do like to imagine that Jesus would've been sitting outside *with* us on that curb, as we wallowed in our little girl guilt and shame, watching us smoke our candy cigarettes. He'd be hanging out with us, holding our little nine-year-old hearts, whispering, "You're okay. You know this isn't really *who* you are anyway."

All of us are wired with rebellion. We are human. I have found in my life that it's like there's this light switch in my heart that turns on rebellion. I can turn it on and I can turn it off. But what determines whether I turn it on or off?

It's my trust in God. It's my willingness to let go and let Him be in control. It's making the choice to see that He knows best, even when everything within me is wrestling to be in control, fighting to get what I want, the way that I want it.

When I don't trust God, that switch comes on. I rebel. I do it for spite. I do it for revenge. I do it for attention. I do it for pride. I do it to make a name for myself. I do it out of my sin nature, which is always more concerned with *self*.

It's not easy to be in alignment with God at all times. Again, we are human. We battle, oftentimes, daily. But it helps me to know that I have a choice. I can point that spray can under the table and shoot, or I can choose to keep it hidden away in my preteen purse. It comes down to the choice of trusting Him. That ball is in my court.

I think back to that day with my cousin and with my aunt. I laugh at the ridiculousness of our rebellion and the way things unfolded, but I also remember that after that episode, my aunt pulled us lovingly aside and reminded us that she is our aunt, and that we belong to her and she loves us. She reminded us that she knows that we *really are* nice, sweet, girls.

When we put our trust in God, when we really choose to let Him lead us, keeping that light switch of rebellion *off* in our lives, He does this amazing thing. He speaks life into us and reminds us that we are His. He reminds us that He loves us. He reminds us of who we *really* are.

And those candy cigarette smoking little girls are just a façade for the real us.

CHAPTER 6

Happy Family

"Happy is the man who finds a true friend, and far happier is he who finds that true friend in his wife." ~ Franz Schubert

Ian, my Swiss brother from another mother, came to visit my family in Texas a few summers ago. He had never been to Texas, and had never met my parents, though I fondly called his American parents my "Euro Parents."

We gave him the full "Anderson Family North Texas Tour," which included a trip to The Trail Dust (known for it's amazing steaks and a three-story slide that lands you plop in the middle of the dance floor) and Six Flags Over Texas (the Mr. Freeze ride and *pink things* are enough to keep me happy for days). We even introduced him to field-grazing Texas longhorns and oil pump jacks. On our last day, we spent time at our famous antique-shopping nook of a square in my hometown of McKinney, followed by delicious pie and sweet tea.

After our adventures together in Texas, Ian made a statement that resonated with me. He said, "Bethany, I've never seen a relationship like your parents have; they are best friends. That's exactly what I want in my life."

I thought about that for a moment. I realized that it had taken me living away from home, under the roofs of various people, and the fresh perspective of a friend to realize the gold and beauty that was right before me my entire life.

It's true. My parents are best friends. They spend more time with each other than with anyone else. They go see independent films on the weekends, and regularly stumble upon free outdoor concerts and cultural events. In fact, I am always receiving random photos by text or email bragging, "Guess where we are?" And sometimes it goes beyond that - I'll get a voicemail of blaring music in the background, with my mom yelling, "Guess who's playing in concert tonight?"

The things they do together don't stop at what most would call *normal*. When I was living at home right after I graduated from Baylor University, I was getting ready to walk out the door to work, when I popped my head into my parents' bedroom. I noticed a stack of suitcases piled on their bed. For some reason that didn't strike me as odd, so I just yelled, "Bye Mom, I'm off to work. See you tonight!" She ran after me and said, "No, wait until your dad gets back so you can tell him goodbye." I was like, "Why? I'll see him tonight." Then she nonchalantly said, "Oh well, we decided to go to South Padre Island today. Didn't you see the bags on the bed?"

I just stared at her with my mouth wide-open. South Padre Island is a twelve-hour drive from our house. You have to drive through Dallas, Waco, Austin, San Antonio, and lots of other smaller towns to get there. They pull stuff like this all the time, though, so I wasn't that shocked. I was just offended they didn't invite me along.

One time they decided to drive from McKinney, Texas to Canada. They spent three weeks out and about on the road just for the heck of it, although they did randomly stop by upstate New York to see my actor friends studying at the prestigious Chautauqua Institute.

Back to my parents' totally normal, spontaneous trip to South Padre - they headed out, spent the night in Austin, and arrived late the next afternoon. When they got to the island, there were absolutely no rooms available because it was Spring Break in Texas - a minor oversight on their parts! Most people would be disheartened by this discovery. Most people would turn around and pick another location, a less Spring-Break-y one. My parents, though, aren't most people.

Instead, they went to dinner, and then found the nearest Walmart on the other side of the bay. They bought a two-person tent and camped out on the beach, next to the boozing and shenanigans of party-going Spring Breakers.

Reflecting on the amazing, fun, and zany marriage that my parents' share makes me extremely grateful for my upbringing. It makes me thankful for parents who value fun and laughter, life, spontaneity, and togetherness.

Despite an incredible example of marriage though, a strange thing happened a couple of years back. I had this stark revelation that I don't have hang-ups about marriage because I hate commitment or because I think my relationship will end in divorce, I have reservations about marriage because I think I'll never be able to imitate the amazing and beautiful friendship that my parents share.

I'm beyond that thought these days (thankfully it was pretty fleeting!), because I have realized, though I'm not married yet, that a marriage is what you make it. If I value humor and laughter and spontaneity and making the most out of every situation, while seeking adventure and life and passion, then that's what I will bring to my marriage. Besides, no marriage is ever perfect. It's a journey.

I know that it's a journey because I have had the uncommon privilege to live with many people. I count my parents in that, obviously, but I have also lived with a family in France, one in Switzerland, and one in South Africa. It's one thing to visit people and stay in their home; it's another thing to *live* there. When you live with someone, there is no hiding the real, raw, and ugly. I've seen it all, and I count it as a beautiful blessing – one that has exposed me to all kinds of relationships. It's been an intensive course in marriage preparation for that day when I finally take that long walk down the aisle.

But until I have my own marriage to build and create, I will sit across the dinner table and watch my parental best friends laugh, prod, and rib each other. I will listen and laugh with them as they come up with the next greatest skits for *Saturday Night Live*. I will sit in the back of the car and observe how my dad gently places his hand on top of my mom's, as he's driving on a long stretch of highway. I will lose my breath laughing from reminiscing about a particular trip to Santa Fe, where my mom told my dad that his socks were ugly. He pulled them off right there at the restaurant bar and threw them into the nearby potted-plant. I will close my eyes and remember the way they celebrated our birthdays with personal candle-lit breakfast treats and loud, off-key renditions of "Happy Birthday" on every birthday morning. I will watch them sit too close on the couch while Dad reads the newspaper, and Mom, her latest novel. I will watch as they dance to Latin beats in the car on the way to meet my brothers and their wives for dinner. I will listen to them argue over whether Britney Spears is worth listening to or not. I will roll my eyes as they do this fake *kissy kissy* thing with lots of sound effects just to get on my nerves.

I will be grateful to God for a model of marriage that is rooted in love and friendship, and until I'm married, I will practice making the most of every moment with the loved ones already in my life.

CHAPTER 7

Heartstrings & Pie

"Memories! How they hurt! My eyes fill with tears,
But only for a moment, then I say goodbye to my fears.
I'll always love you, my soul mate of years.
How can I ever forget you, my love and dear?"
~ Dot Crosswhite, poem to my grandfather, September 10, 1994

Because I have lived overseas for so many of my adult years, I make it a top priority to spend time with my grandmother, Dot, when I'm home in Texas. She's my only living grandparent, and we have weekly grandmother-granddaughter dates.

Usually we go out for lunch, but lately we've been doing projects around Dot's house. Recently, we've framed magazine cut-outs into the shape of a cross, canned peaches, painted old frames, and pickled beets.

Not too long ago, we baked a pineapple coconut cake for our upcoming family reunion. And while we were waiting for the buzzer on the oven timer, we sipped our sweet tea and discussed the origin of my grandmother's love for sweets.

Dot grew up on a farm in central Texas, and with four siblings and little money, big meals were scarce. Even in the tough times, though, my great-grandmother would bake a pie. As a young girl, my grandmother says she only got a tiny sliver of pie. To demonstrate, as she always does when she tells this story, she dramatically takes her fingers, putting them in the shape of a very small triangle, wrinkles her forehead and stares at me with a glimmer in her eye until I nod in agreement, "Yes, yes, that *is* a small piece of pie!" (I said this with as much gusto as possible so she'd understand that I do believe a world with no pie is a sad one, indeed.) Because of this mealtime tradition, my grandmother always dreamed of eating pie. Literally. She's told me stories of childhood nights, with her head on the pillow, thinking and drooling about mouth-watering pie.

So, ninety-three years later, she eats as much pie as she likes. She's making up for lost time, I suppose. In fact, just last week I was visiting with her over a meal and she hardly ate any of her food, complaining that she wasn't really hungry anymore. Not two minutes later, the waiter walked up to clear her plate, and she said, "I'll have a slice of chocolate pie, please."

These types of encounters always make me laugh because I definitely inherited her sweet tooth. Although I haven't succumbed to eating chocolate icing on my toast yet as a replacement to Nutella like she does, that time will come, I'm sure.

Anyway, after our long conversation about the challenges of a childhood without much pie, my grandmother looked over at me and said, "I want to tell you something. Do you mind?" I was taken aback by this question because she is private about the details of her life. She comes from the generation that doesn't like to over-share or pry or even *almost* over-share or pry. This question shifted the atmosphere in the room.

I told her to "Go ahead," and tuned-in to a story that danced out of her mouth like a melodic dirge.

She said that the day that my grandfather died in 1993, he had invited her to go pick some vegetables in their garden at their farm, about twenty miles outside of town. She had decided that day that she would be more productive working on her flower garden at the house, and that he should go on without her, making sure to return by 5pm. Though he normally took his little black dog companion, R.P., with him for farm work, he decided to leave him with my grandmother because he had been acting strange recently.

So off my grandfather went. Later in the day, as my grandmother was pulling up some weeds, she felt a sharp pain fluttering in her heart. She told me that she literally felt like her heart was wrapped in string and someone was tugging it with force and violence, stealing her breath with each tug. She ran inside and drank a tall glass of water to settle her nerves and ease the pain. She thought she was having a heart attack, but then the pain subsided and left her feeling discombobulated and off-kilter. Despite this, she went back to finish the work in her garden until my grandfather returned.

But he never did.

She reckons that moment of heart torture was the exact moment when my grandfather, Buddy, fell off his tractor to his death.

She said, "Bethany, I always thought heartstrings sounded like a poetic cliché, but I know they are real."

I sat there with tears warming my eyes, pondering the stories of hope and heartache hiding behind the wrinkles on the beautiful face before me.

My grandmother has taught me many things, but that day I saw a depth of pain, redeemed by the flickering light of joy in her eyes. I realized that we are all attached by heartstrings, and because we are spiritual beings, we are connected to one another beyond what any of us can even begin to imagine. Love transcends the physical and attaches us to one another through the supernatural, through God.

My grandmother is one of my closest friends and I'm privileged to have had so many precious moments with her. She's one of the strongest women I know. She's been through more emotional pain than one should endure in a lifetime – she's lost parents, siblings, a husband, two infant sons, two grown sons to cancer, and two grandchildren to ill health and tragedy. She never wavers in her faith, though. She keeps her eyes fixed on God, and beams a smile brighter than the sun every time she sees me.

She's pretty unpredictable, too, which I have also inherited from her. In fact, several years ago, we were sitting in my parents' kitchen after my uncle, her third son, had passed away from leukemia. We were chatting around the table with some aunts and cousins, snacking and sipping on sweet tea (again), and out of nowhere she pulls out this tiny gold ring and hands it to me. She said, "Bethany, I want you to have this ring. It was from my engagement." I was honored and said, "This is your engagement ring from Buddy?"

She said, "No, it's my engagement ring from Samuel Goldberger."

You could hear a pin drop in that moment, until my aunt, cousins, and I screamed in confused unison, breaking the silence: "WHAT?

You were engaged before?"

She coyly batted her eyelashes as she answered a simple, "Yes," followed by deafening silence. After a barrage of questions from her audience of family members who had now encircled her like hungry wolves, she proceeded to tell us the details of her engagement to a young Jewish man when she was living and working as an optical nurse in New York City.

Not one person in my family knew this story - not my mom or any of her four brothers. We were totally dumb-founded.

Then there's the story of Perry. After my grandfather passed away, my grandmother spent time with one of his old work colleagues, who was a fellow widower. They became fast companions and spent lots of time together doing errands, sharing meals, and taking day-trips to nearby local towns.

Then one day, Perry just disappeared. When our family asked what happened to him, all my grandmother would chirp was, "He was a pest. I sent him away."

We later learned that she told him never to call her again because he was too clingy and it suffocated her freedom and independence

That was about twenty years ago. Well, fast-forward to a couple of months ago and my grandmother was sitting at home watching TV and the phone rang. She has caller-ID and is very particular about which calls she answers.

She didn't get a good read on the caller-ID this particular day and picked up the phone to say, " Hello?" The voice on the other end of the line said, "Hello Dot. This is Perry."

Knowing exactly who it was, my grandmother let the silence between them thicken, and then said, "Larry?"

"No, Perry."

"Gary?"

"No, Perry."

"Harry?"

"Well, shoot," and Perry slammed the phone down.

I have a very vivid mental image of her repeating this story to me as she sat in the front seat of my blue Subaru. She cackled, rocking back and forth in uncontrollable laughter while recounting the story, as tears streamed down her cheeks. I literally thought she was losing her mind.

She then looked at me and winked, much like a child who has gotten away with pulling a prank on their parents and said, "I did it! He thinks I'm crazy! He'll never bother me again!"

The more time I spend with my grandmother, the more I see myself in her. In fact, her baby boy, my uncle, likes to tell me every time he sees me, "Bethany, you are just like your grandmother. Crazy."

I take this as an absolute compliment. She is a little bit crazy, a little bit unpredictable, and a whole lot feisty. I love my grandmother, and it is an honor for someone to tell me that I'm like her.

Just as she thinks of my grandfather when she thinks of *heartstrings*, I think of *her*.

I think about God, too, sometimes like I think about my grandmother. Maybe He's not addicted to pie and sweet tea, and maybe He doesn't play pranks on crazy old men (or maybe He does!), but He is unpredictable. The biggest compliment anyone can give me is to say that some part of me resembles God somehow. I want to be like Him, I want to spend as much time with Him as possible, and I want my *heartstrings* to be attached to His more than anyone or anything else.

---

*Since I wrote this story, my sweet grandmother, Dot, went to be with Jesus on August 29, 2017. I was blessed to spend her final days with her by her bedside, along with my mom, uncles, and other family members. We all promised her that we'd eat pie in her honor at every holiday gathering. I also made her promise that she'd help God find me a husband when she came face-to-face with Him.

The day she passed I wrote this:

I'm so thankful to God for giving me seven solid days to minister love over my precious grandmother through songs and scriptures, prayers, laughter and tears. As I left her bedside last night and sensed that God would finally call her home, I anointed her with frankincense oil and whispered into her ear one last time: "Run wild & free into Jesus' presence! Run wild and free!" Several days prior, I asked God to give me a sign when she was about to pass. He was gracious, and right after falling asleep this morning just after midnight, I awoke and saw a vision of Dot lying on her bed swirled in beautiful, vibrant colors, all while encompassed by a glorious angel of light. Shortly thereafter, we got a call and were told that she had passed onto eternity at 1:50 am. Dot IS NOW running wild & free with Jesus!

Dot was more than a grandmother to me – she was a best friend. The older I get, the more I realize that we are the same. I am my grandmother – an admirer of all things bright and beautiful, a lover of creatures great and small, and a wild spirit set on blazing new trails and chasing adventures with God!

CHAPTER 8

The Day of Whales

"Praise the LORD *from the earth, you great sea creatures and all ocean depths… wild animals and all cattle, small creatures and flying birds…"* ~ *Psalm 148:7,10 (NIV)*
"Beauty is God's handwriting." ~ *Charles Kingsley*

I recently spent a week with my soul-twin, Kerstin, out in California thawing out from a crazy Texas winter and searching for moments of peace, quiet, and rest for my soul. On my fourth morning, I awoke to an energetic post-bike-ride Kerstin who greeted me with enthusiasm. She told me about her ride down to the ocean to spend time with God and how, as she was praying, she peered out into the ocean to see two whales just off the coast.

I smiled with glee in an effort to live vicariously through her amazing encounter that morning, but also playfully declared, "I, too, will see a whale today in Jesus' Name! Amen." She played along and gave her nod of approval, "Amen."

Deep within me is a desire to connect with nature. Listening to waves slap the sand while smelling the fresh tinge of salt in the air, all while watching the tide dance with the earth inspires me and takes me to a so-called other place. However, I find I am most overwhelmed with God's goodness when I encounter creatures in the wild.

Part of the time that I worked as a missionary in South Africa, I lived on the shores of False Bay. This is the infamous territory of the Great White shark, made famous by the popular Discovery channel TV series, *Shark Week*. I would start my mornings in my living room, hot tea in hand, overlooking the sun poking through my window. I would examine the horizon in hopes of seeing some sort of creature lift its head out of the water or expose its fin as if to wave "hello," even for a fleeting moment.

Some days I had better success than others. One morning, I saw several seals synchronized swimming across the calm of the ocean. On another occasion, in the cove directly across from my window, I saw a mother whale tending to her baby.

Just a five-minute drive down the road, I could visit the African penguins of Boulder's Beach anytime I wanted. Considering that I had an ongoing competition with my Texas pastor about who could serendipitously stumble across the most animals in their natural habitats, this seemed a little bit like cheating. But nonetheless, I would visit my favorite little penguins as much as possible. I frequented Boulder's Beach so often that I even became deluded, thinking that the little waddling tuxedos might begin to recognize me and run to me, flippers flapping in the wind, offering me a cuddly penguin hug.

I even had several encounters with baboons during my time in South Africa. My aforementioned Texas pastor was in the country doing a seminar on his latest book, and it was my job to show him the beautiful sights of the Cape Town region. As part of our tour, we traveled to Cape Point to stare at the end of the earth. As we drove along the road and chatted through life, ministry, and funny cultural mishaps, I suddenly slammed on the brakes. To my surprise, there was an entire baboon troop blocking the path! They were in no hurry to get out of the way of traffic. In fact, I remember a particular cheeky little guy walking right down the middle of the road, as if to say, "Stop. *I'm* king of the road." We spent twenty minutes slowly scooting toward our destination. I didn't complain though, because I was too busy laughing the entire time at our hilarious front-row view: pink, baby baboon butt-cheeks mooning us while riding atop its mother's shoulders.

The next day with my pastor ushered in another *creature in the wild* encounter. We went to my favorite local surf-spot, Muizenberg. We rented boards for a midday surf and took the plunge into the frigid waters. After catching several waves, I was on my final ride into shore. As I pulled myself up and steadied my footing on my waxy long board, I focused my gaze towards the shoreline. My concentration was broken when, out of the water three inches in front of my surfboard, leapt a wet, shiny baby seal. I immediately dove off my board and, upon resurfacing screamed to my pastor, "Look! Look! It's a baby seal!" He jumped off his board and fought the current to chase after the seal. He eventually gave up once he realized he'd been out-swum by a creature that swims for a living!

That day was one of the most beautiful and profound moments of my life. As a worship leader, I often connect with God and, therefore, lead others to connect with God through musical worship. I would easily say, though, that my encounter with the seal that day was one of the most depth-filled, stirring moments of worship I've ever experienced. It released a level of praise and thankfulness in me that I didn't even know existed. I sat on the shore after that, overtaken by a flood of emotions and gratitude. I felt so loved by such a creative Creator.

I had a similar worship-evoking encounter when I lived in Australia. From the moment I stepped foot onto Australian soil, my selfish prayer was, "Please Jesus, let me see a koala in the wild while I'm here!" I uttered that same prayer every so often throughout my time in Bible College in Australia, because I know God loves to bless us in the small things, and I desperately wanted to see His creation in its natural element. That would be such an incredible gift.

He answered that prayer over and over again in the form of wild kangaroos, but not koalas. During my years there, I saw countless kangaroos in peoples' front yards, on university campuses, and hopping down random roads. Though I was extremely grateful for these sightings, my heart still yearned to see a cuddly koala.

God didn't overlook my little prayer. During the last couple of weeks leading up to my move back to the USA, I took a road trip along the Great Ocean Road with some close friends. As we were deep in conversation, rounding the bend through the tropical rain forest terrain, I blurted out to Carmen, my South African friend, who was on driving duty at the moment, "Stop! There he is! There's *my* koala!"

Fortunately, there was a tiny spot off the road to pull over. Without delay before the car had come to a complete stop, I flung the door open and jumped out with my camera in hot pursuit of my koala friend. He was drunk on Eucalyptus leaves and was sauntering out of the bush area at a snail's pace. This allowed me to casually creep up behind him with my camera, shooting his every move as he sleepily dawdled along in search of another napping spot. At one point, he turned and looked at me, almost with a glint in his eye as if to say, "I'm yours!" I followed him under a low-lying branch into the tropical flora, but after being poked and stabbed by several exotic plants, I threw in the cards on my stalking efforts. I told my friend goodbye as he walked away and I thanked God for introducing us. My friends can testify to the fact that I was smiling ear to ear and fighting back happy tears for the rest of the day.

Again, this encounter with a creature in the wild released something within me. I felt it was God's special gift to me, a way for Him to come alongside me and say, "I see you. I know you. And I want to give you my best!"

All this brings me back to my thawing-out retreat in California with my friend, Kerstin. After she regaled me with her story about seeing two whales just off the coastline, we loaded in the car and headed south to meet a longtime friend for dinner. Because the ocean makes us both feel so alive, and because I currently live in North Texas and she lives in the cement city of London, we decided it would be completely worthwhile to take Highway One, the slow but scenic ocean-side route.

Kerstin once again talked me through her encounter with God and the whales. As I listened, I locked my eyes on the horizon across the water, in hopes of seeing my own personal whale.

Not five minutes later, I shouted, "There he is! There he is! It's *my* whale! Pull over!" Kerstin stopped the car with skills that would make James Bond jealous. We leapt out of the car and quickly realized that it wasn't just one whale, or even two, but there were at least four whales off the coast in front of us. She laughed and said, "I think the whales are following me!" I retorted with, "No, they are showing off for *me*!"

We giggled like the little schoolgirls we sometimes wish we still were, and began to praise our Creator God. I'm pretty sure the Asian man sitting in the parked car in front of us thought we were crazy, but we didn't care. God had gifted us with whales, lots of whales! We stood there going on and on and on about the goodness of God, and eventually had to force ourselves back onto the road so we wouldn't totally miss daylight or our dinner date with our friend.

But the story doesn't end there.

As we drove along Highway One for the next two and a half hours, we literally began to lose count of the whales we saw. The water was extremely calm and, therefore, gave us the ability to see miles out to sea, where we could catch glimpses of whale-spouts dancing against the horizon. Sometimes we saw single travelers, and other times we saw a symphonic chorus of four to six whales each. Their spouts sprayed like beautiful fountains with the romantic backdrop of a shimmering sun.

This moment of connection with God's beautiful chorus of whales caused our praise to rise up out of us like glistening fountains, too.

I believe with the core of my being that these simple prayers I have prayed in my past are not selfish, as they may seem at first. When I cry out to see a creature in the wild, it's because I know the wild creature in me needs to be released, inspired, set free to praise. God knows I have a well of praise bubbling in my soul, and sometimes, it's these little gifts He gives me, which spark that praise deep within me. I don't know why that is. Maybe it's because from my earliest memories, I have been an animal lover. Maybe it's because every unique creation is a reminder of His beauty and creativity as the Ultimate Designer.

I may not totally understand why I am so moved and shaken when I see creatures in the wild, but I do know that's exactly how God created me. He created me to love and adore His Creation. And He created me to love and adore Him, the Creator.

He is the perfect Artist. He doesn't make mistakes. He never puts a dot where a cross is supposed to be, and He never paints with black and white when color would work better. He knows. He orchestrates. He designs.

Even though my friend and I just happened to pick dates on a calendar when our busy travel schedules seemed to mesh, God orchestrated all of this. He knew I needed a friend that week. He knew I needed a whale. And most importantly, He knew I needed Him above all else.

CHAPTER 9

Collecting Stories

"Therefore, accept each other just as Christ has accepted you so that God will be given glory." ~ Romans 15:7 (NLV)

There's something thrilling about traveling the world on your own. It's probably just the way I'm wired, because I have lots of friends who would strongly disagree with that statement. In fact, I've had several friends at different times in my life say something along the lines of, "I don't know how you travel alone. I could never do that. I'd be too scared." I try to understand their fear, but I never really do because I don't see traveling alone as actually being *alone*. One of the reasons I love it so much is because there are people everywhere. There are people that are just like your closest friends and family, even people like your strange college roommate or your crazy Uncle Bob. I am energized and hypnotized by the types of people that I meet along the way from point A to point B, and even more captivated by the idea of collecting stories everywhere I go. I have a world-adventuring tradition with my parents. They always chauffeur me to the Dallas/Fort Worth International Airport, park the car in one-hour parking, and escort me inside to make sure I get all my bags checked-in. Once I have my passport and boarding pass in my hands, and I have rustled through my bag to reorganize things in preparation for the rigorous security process, I turn to my mom and dad to say my goodbyes. After a couple of rounds of hugs and "I love yous," I walk towards the security line to the tune of the emboldening words I've heard on the brink of every adventure I've ever embarked upon: "Go collect stories!"

I love meeting new people so much; in fact, there is a lot I will do/sacrifice/compromise for a good story. Don't get me wrong - I'm not willing to compromise my moral standards and I'm not mindless about it. After many years of global travel, I have fined-tuned my "discernment radar." With that said, I will start a conversation with someone out-of-the-blue just to get to know her story. It's always worth it to me, because the best stories come from the people that are walking down the street beside us or sitting on public transportation next to us.

I was at a training seminar in California recently, and had several story-worthy encounters with strangers. The first one happened shortly after I boarded my shuttle from the airport to downtown Los Angeles. The long-haired Florida native in front of me, turned to face me in the seat directly behind him, and pointedly asked me, "Hey, where's the best weed in LA?" As the shock dissipated from my face, I started laughing and said, "Do I look like I know where the best weed in LA is?" He just silently stared at me, and turned to face forward again. I surveyed my attire and appearance to see what about me would lead him to believe that I knew such information. Maybe it was the fact that I was dressed in my typical "hippie" style, but in any case, I wasn't sure if this was a compliment - like, "You're cool" or an insult, "She looks like a pothead." Either way, I was glad he asked me, because even though I know nothing about weed, have never smoked it, and never will, it was a point of connection between two people. Our interaction was an open door for further conversation (after I recovered from the shock of the question) and my new friend, Brad, taught me that there's something so simply profound about human contact: we just have to open our mouths and talk to one another. We could have sat in our shuttle, among strangers, checking our phones and keeping to ourselves. But, we didn't. We chatted. We engaged with one another.

Sometimes I think we've forgotten what it's like to talk to people we don't know. We grew up being told by our parents, "Don't talk to strangers." That makes sense when you're teaching a small child safe boundaries with people. Unfortunately, though, that has resulted in a habit where, even as adults, we don't talk to strangers. Of course the world we live in is scary, crazy, and unpredictable. People can be that way, too, but I know I've missed out on a lot of life by keeping my mouth shut and not engaging with others at times. My trip reminded me that people want to talk, open up, and even *want* to be asked.

My second encounter was with a beautiful soul named Amelia.

She was a yogini master, who had lost vision in her left eye because she used to stand on her head for such long periods of time. She told me excitedly, "I get such a thrill from being upside down!" She sat next to me in the training seminar I was attending, and regaled me with snippets of life stories, both sweet and shocking. We connected on a heart-level immediately and became best buddies during the conference. We dined together daily and swapped stories like US Dollars for Euros at a currency exchange. I learned intimate details about the struggles of her family life and about her move across the country. She was open and vulnerable, and with every conversation, the threads of connection weaved us more tightly together. Reflecting on my time with Amelia, I think fondly about the imprint she left on my heart: she inspired me to see the beauty in all things, despite the pain and hardship. Her stories caused me to rejoice that God's kingdom is at hand; He is at work in and through all people, all conversations, and all circumstances. If we open our eyes wide enough to see Him at work, we will, and when we do, we can see that when God is involved, nothing is in vain. Ever.

My third encounter happened late on a Thursday night in Hollywood. My fellow training program attendees had no interest in venturing out to see the sites of Los Angeles, so I gusto-ed up the gumption to go by myself. I ordered an Uber taxi and treated myself to a vegan dinner at Tender Greens on Sunset Boulevard, followed by two comedy shows at the IO West.

After the comedy show ended, I strolled solo down Hollywood Boulevard to Grauman's Chinese Theater. It probably wasn't the smartest idea, as I was the only single female walking the street that late, but I did my best to "draft" behind cuddly couples to look like I was sauntering as part of a group. Though I picked-up many sideways glances and catcalls along the way, I was only taunted once verbally. The eleven-minute walk seemed to last for eternity, but, thankfully, I felt God's presence with me the whole time.

Once I had the Chinese Theater in sight, I crossed the street into freedom, an area full of other tourists. As I crossed the street, I noticed a tall, trendy looking guy watching me. I thought nothing of it, and kept walking to document my visit to the Theater on Instagram. As soon as I turned to take a picture, that same tall, trendy looking guy was standing right next to me.

He blurted out, "Excuse me, do you know a good vegan restaurant around here?"

This question caught me off-guard for a few reasons: 1. This guy was pigeonholing me as a vegan, 2. I had actually *just* eaten at a vegan restaurant (which I never do) and 3. It was an odd request because it was really late at night. I eventually recovered from my surprise and turned to him and said, "Actually, I just ate at a really good vegan restaurant called Tender Greens," and proceeded to tell him the location and detailed directions on how to find it.

This unexpected interaction led to further banter. It turned out that Tom, this vegan-fare-searching guy, was actually *from* LA. When I realized this, I asked him why he asked me for a restaurant recommendation when he was a local. He claimed to be doing a survey of people on the street, in search of a good restaurant for his friend that he was meeting. He also mentioned that the way I was dressed screamed, "Vegan." I laughed again. This was the second time in a short four-day period where I was stereotyped by the way I looked – first as a weed connoisseur, and then as a vegan. (I'm sensing a theme here.)

The "vegan" conversation led to rabbit trails of various shapes, sizes, and destinations. I spent about ninety minutes with Hollywood Tom as my local tour guide. He showed me the Chinese Theater and then gave me a tour of the Hotel Roosevelt just across the street, including the bowling, secret pool, and garden terrace. This portion of my evening with a random stranger quickly escalated me to the peak of my spontaneity and impulsivity.

My mom will probably cringe reading about Hollywood Tom, mostly because she'll be wondering how in the world she birthed a daughter who fears only two things: tornadoes and lightning. She'll be wondering why I have no fear when it comes to venturing out on my own or meeting new people from various walks of life. She'll wonder why taking an Uber in downtown Los Angeles doesn't freak me out, and why I would ever consider walking the streets of Sunset or Hollywood Boulevard on my own late at night. This isn't to imply that she's a fearful person – she's absolutely not, but she *can be* fearful for *me*. I'm a little bit like the black sheep in my family. I'm dangerously independent. But more than that, I'm dangerously attracted to people. I love to meet diverse people with stories of all colors and forms, and at the expense of my own comfort or desires, I'll go along with a situation (using discernment, of course) just for a good story.

Here's the thing: I think Jesus was just the same. He went out of His way walking on seas, hiking through valleys, tiptoeing through deserts, searching in trees and resting at wells, collecting stories of the people all around Him. He looked at them face-to-face, eyeball-to-eyeball and connected with them. He *saw* them. He listened to their stories. He answered their questions. He became community for them. He was a safe place of light, joy, love, and refuge. And after meeting them, His story became their story.

I want the same. I want people to experience Jesus through my life. I want my eyes to communicate His love, His life, and His light. I want to speak hope and faith over people's stories. I want to see redemption come. I want to see healing abound. I want to see joy exuded. I want to connect people to the love of Jesus.

I so desperately want Florida Brad, Yogini Amelia, Hollywood Tom, and everyone everywhere to know the unconditional love and grace of Jesus. Sometimes that just starts with opening our mouths and talking to one another.

CHAPTER 10

<u>Kiss My Fish</u>

"This is a quaint little drinking village with a fishing problem."
~ Sign on the wall of Beach & Station Street Grill in Port Aransas, Texas

Every summer, my family spends a week on the beach just off the coast of Texas in a quaint fishing village called Port Aransas. In January of 2013, I was about to embark upon a new adventure, which would land me in a really cold climate indefinitely, so I begged my parents for a last-chance getaway to the beach to prep me for the months ahead.

The three of us traveled to Port Aransas and stayed in my cousin's condo for a wonderful winter Texas break. Though the air was a bit chilly, the sun was out to keep us company for the entirety of our stay.

Per our normal summer routine, we ventured out one night to one of our favorite island restaurants, Beach & Station Street Grill. We were seated at a table in close proximity to a makeshift bar, as well as the neighboring table. I sat closest to that table and could have easily rested my left elbow on it, while still comfortably seated at mine. The place was very small, but packed with all sorts of local characters.

After about five minutes there, we were sharing the same close breathing space as one of those local characters. Pete came strutting into the small restaurant, his hair wet with salt and his skin the color and texture of brown leather. He wore a T-shirt promoting what I later learned to be his favorite adult beverage. A similarly leather-looking lady named Barb sat across the table from him as he took the seat nearest to me, overtaking my previous elbow rest.

I attempted to pay no attention to their conversation, which proved quite difficult since we were seated within arms distance of each other. I was somewhat successful at this aim until Pete started slurring demands at our waiter. "Bring me a plate, man. I don't want no fancy big plate. Bring me a small plate, now. Hurry up you *bleep*!"

(Note: From hence forth, there will be a lot of "bleeps." If you are offended that I would even be retelling a story that involves so many "bleeps," kindly move on to the next chapter.)

This blatant yelling caught me off-guard, and from that moment forward, my ears were tuned to the conversation at my neighboring table. Pete and Barb glassily gazed into each other's eyes and held hands under the table. They shared an appetizer of fried shrimp and, though they gave the air of a *lovey-dovey* relationship, their words to one another were sharp and jagged like a hunter's knife.

"Where's my *bleep* napkin, Barb? Did you steal it?"

"No, Pete, just shut the *bleep* up and eat your shrimp."

"No, Barb. Now my fingers are sticky and it's all your fault."

This kind of loving and gentle banter went on for several minutes and as I took my first bite of my pre-dinner salad, the waiter arrived with their meals: one plate of blackened snapper and one plate of grilled snapper.

I was chatting with my parents, whom were both sitting to my right, about something when I was shocked out of conversation and into shaking fear. Pete had taken the previously asked-for small plate and violently slammed it down on our table, right in front of my newly adopted elbow space. I tensed-up, not sure what violent act might follow.

Then Pete got right in my face and slurred, "Ya want some fish? We caught it this afternoon out on the Gulf."

Once I recovered from my initial shock at this unexpected interaction and offer of kindness, I sheepishly said, "No, but thank you very much." I should've kept my big trap shut, but stupidly I continued, "I don't like fish."

In that moment, Pete thrashed his body away from mine and then snapped back around to burn a hole into me with his beady, pointed eyes: "YOU don't like fish? You DON'T like fish? YOU DON'T LIKE FISH?!?!?" With every repetition of the phrase, he grew louder and more passionate, moving closer and closer until he was spitting his judgment right onto my reddened cheeks.

Then with a major flair of drama, he made eye contact yet again and said, "Well, you can kiss... my... fish!!! KISS. *MY*. FISH."

(Note: Pete did not really use the word "fish" here, but I've replaced that other kind of expletive so that we can all be happy about this story.)

To ease the tension, my mom leaned across me and batted her eyelashes at Pete, "I'd love to try some fish."

Bitter Pete dished some up and put it on our table, giving me the evil eye as he forcefully slid it away from me and towards my parents. Then he went back to his not-so-romantic evening with Barb.

Guilt completely overtook me and I decided that I should give that deep-water snapper a fair shake, so I took a bite. It was one of the most delicious things I have ever tasted! It also tasted a little bit like chicken, which is my go-to protein of choice. My mom quietly asked me if I liked it and I intentionally turned my back towards Pete and faced her, whispering that it was actually delicious and also reminded me of chicken.

A few minutes later, Pete turned back to our table to conduct research on how his fish tasted. I told him that I tried it and that it was really good, obviously and very strategically omitting the part about it tasting like chicken, for fear of Pete's unpredictable response.

After my mom gave her glowing report of the fish, she smiled widely and said to Pete, "My daughter said it tastes like chicken."

Once again Pete thrashed his body away from me like a wild animal and then turned to spit his offense in my direction, "Chicken? ChickEN? CHICKEN?!?" I'm pretty sure at this point I was shaking in my flip-flops.

Here it comes...

"Well, you can Kiss My Fish... KISS MY FISH! CHICKEN?!? KISS MY FISH, LADY!"

The following cannot be made up. Not more than thirty seconds later, our very timely waiter interrupted this back-and-forth heated exchange with the arrival of our food. Plate in hand, he looks at me and says, "Did you order the chicken?"

Yes, that's right. I had ordered chicken-fried chicken at a fish restaurant.

At this point my parents, as well as every single other patron in the restaurant that night started guffawing. They weren't just laughing. They were ugly, snotty, snorty laughing. Well, everybody but Pete that is. He stood up from his table and turned his back towards me in defeat, then sat down again to finish his blackened snapper. I got the hint. He didn't approve of my chicken-loving, fish-rejecting-self causing such a ruckus in his local dive.

In the aftermath of my crazy encounter with my leathered friend, Pete, I was reminded of an important faith lesson. Just because something isn't my first preference or, isn't perhaps even on my radar of preferences, doesn't mean it's not something that I will like or even love. I know that in moments when I think I know what's right and best, I am usually wrong, especially when it comes to understanding God's ways.

In fact, sometimes I wonder if God runs out of patience with me. I know He doesn't. He can't. But because I'm human and frequently run out of patience, I convince myself that God does, too. Surely He wants to scream at me sometimes like Pete, "YOU DON'T LIKE FISH?" Because all the while He's thinking, I am giving this wonderful, delicious gift to you. I created it. I orchestrated it. I know what's best for you and you aren't even willing to try it because the only thing you can think about is what you've always known, *chicken*.

My stubbornness at times is beyond what I can even bear myself. Wouldn't it be much easier if we could just take an eraser and wipe away all of our ugly humanity? Start fresh. Start clean. Well, that's what Jesus is really about. He wants to give us fish. But all we care about is the chicken that we think hits the spot.

I love chicken, don't get me wrong. But when my appetite for life is so aimed at all I know, all I've ever known, or all I think I *will* ever know, I might be missing something God wants to put in front of me. I had a friend once tell me that you can't receive anything from God with closed hands. When we grasp so tightly to the things that we know and think are best, we miss out on a posture of openness before God. We miss out on the delicacies, the new tastes, the mouth-watering flavors he wants us to discover and experience with

Him.

I think back to my senior year of high school. Right before graduation, my small group leader asked us to write about where we saw ourselves in ten years. I remember struggling with this activity. *How do I know where I'll be when I'm twenty-eight?* After several minutes passed, though, I scribbled on the blank piece of paper taunting me, "Married with 2.5 children, living in a house with a white picket fence."

I knew in that moment that I didn't actually believe that. I knew that wasn't what I wanted, but I also knew that it's all I could *see*. I didn't have a cultural framework or lens at eighteen years of age that allowed me to see anything else. It was my "chicken."

Fast-forward ten years to May of 2008, when I was actually twenty-eight years old: I was a single missionary serving the international au pair community in Geneva, Switzerland. I had already lived abroad in France in 2003 as an au pair, and was currently wrapping up my ministry of discipleship and relational evangelism - one of the richest, most flavorful seasons of my life. I shudder to think what my life would've looked like had I been so intent on sticking with the "chicken" that I had always known when God called me to ministry in Switzerland in 2005. I'm thankful for His grace and the Holy Spirit's voice that led me to be *open* to at least try the "fish" God was placing in front of me. It turned out to be better than anything I could've ever dreamed or imagined for my life.

Considering all the heated interaction with Pete about fish and poultry that winter day in Port Aransas, he actually seemed to cool off a bit after indulging in more of his favorite adult beverage. So much so, that he turned to our table and started asking questions about us, including an inquisition on whether or not I was in school or if I was working.

My dad, who at this point had not spoken a word, only managing to snort out several audible laughs, turned to Pete and said, "Oh, let me answer this question. Her nickname is *Baby Preacher Girl.*" I just rolled my eyes at my dad – a silent attempt to communicate, "Please don't egg this man on any further!"

Again Pete made a dramatic move with his body language and looked me square in the eyes: "Let me tell you something, *Baby*

Preacher Girl. I'll live my life the way I want to live my life and you live your life the way you want to live yours. I won't tell you how to live yours, and you won't tell me how to live mine."

And with that, Pete stood from his table, after already having rejected Barb's offer for a bite of her key lime pie. She interjected, "But Pete, you love their key lime pie. Sit down and eat some."

To that Pete responded, "No, Barb. I'm going to go have my favorite dessert which is sitting in a case waiting for me in the Jeep."

Barb finished her pie, profusely apologized for Pete's behavior throughout the course of the evening, and walked out of the restaurant. As soon as the bell rang signifying the closure of the door, the waiter walked out again and said to the three guys sitting above our table at the makeshift bar, "Chicken?"

All three guys had ordered chicken in a fish restaurant, too.

J. BETHANY ANDERSON

GONE EAST: France, Switzerland, The United Kingdom, & The Netherlands

Chapter 11

To Be Known

"It is strange to be known so universally and yet to be so lonely."
~ Albert Einstein

There is such a fine line between aloneness and loneliness. As I type this, I am holed away in my aunt and uncle's spectacular Coloradan mountainside log cabin, completely alone. There is no one within a one-mile radius from here, and zero domesticated animals to keep me company. The closest thing that resembles company is a family of chipmunks that inhabits the porch perimeters, as well as the deer, moose, black bears, and other creatures that are probably stalking me through the window right now.

It's scary to be so alone. The silence of solitude can be maddening, especially when it is interrupted by the shocking noises of odd creaks and bumps in the house. And then there's the problem of the noise in my mind. So many *what if* questions formulate in my head, and eventually pop-out as audible self-talk. Being completely alone, without anyone around, is not something that I'm accustomed to nor is it something I prefer for more than like three days at a time. And that's probably stretching it!

But don't get me wrong; I love being alone. In fact, I find it very freeing and liberating. I love walking the streets of Paris by myself, so that I can set my own pace, stopping and pondering wherever and whenever I like. I can sit and eat my *pain au chocolat* or I can savor it while peeking into my favorite stationery store off *Rue des Rennes*. I also love traveling alone - experiencing new sights and new flavors, as well as eating at restaurants alone. I like going to movies alone. I like driving alone.

I just like to be alone *around people.*

In September of 2003 when I was living and working in Europe as an au pair, I traveled from Geneva, Switzerland to Saint Malo, France completely on my own. This was the first time I had ventured across two countries by myself, and the first time I'd be staying solo in a hotel room, exploring a new city, and tasting the local cuisine by myself. More than that, I had a Swiss phone that didn't work in France, so I was "off-grid" for the entire weekend. I remember the fear of total separation from those I loved, as well as those who counted on me daily, and yet I experienced this electrifying exhilaration. *I can do this. I can travel the world on my own!*

My experience in France taught me that I like being by myself, just not completely alone. Because with all of these adventures, there's always been someone nearby, perhaps at the next table, or in the seat next to me laughing in unison at the funny parts of the movie, or making that same frustrated snarl as we sit bumper-to-bumper in traffic. There's always someone else in the café or on the bus, or taking pictures on the seawall. There's always someone working at the hotel desk, or behind the counter at the quaint shop, or stamping my train ticket.

I didn't grow up in a big city, but I have learned through my travels that I have a big city mentality. I like noise and clutter and culture and variety and the quick pace of city life.

And yet, here's what I find ironic: we can be surrounded by people, whether by our parents, our children, spouse, housemates, friends, family or even strangers, and yet, still feel lonely. We can have all the love in the world and still feel the pang of loneliness that rots away at the core of our very souls.

I've often wondered why that is, but reflecting on my solo travels, jumping from country to country, I have pinpointed what I think it is. I often experienced the pit of loneliness when I feel the most vulnerable, misunderstood, or when I feel that no one really knows me or cares to know me.

I had this thought recently about our culture's collective fascination with celebrities. Honestly, I am disgusted by my own interest in the nitty-gritty details of the lives of people that I don't even know, and, in most cases, don't even find that interesting. But for whatever reason, we are drawn to celebrity news like moths to a flame. We watch them on reality TV shows, we follow their blogs, we peruse their Tweets, and we scour the magazines from cover-to-cover to peer voyeuristically into their lives.

Although I personally try to avoid getting sucked into this trap for fear of meaningless celebrity knowledge taking up more of my limited brain capacity, there is something very fundamentally human about our obsession with celebrities.

And that's this: God created us to be *known*.

Because we live in a social-media saturated world, we are a generation that chases fame more than any other generation that has gone before us. I believe that this focused energy on fame and celebrity status is simply because our hearts deeply desire for people to see, know, and understand us. God created us so that we would be known by Him, and so that we would be known by others. That's what community is all about, knowing and being known.

And so when I think about those lonely seasons in my life, I think it's because I feel like no one really understands what I am feeling, no one understands my battles, and in terms of living abroad, no one knows where I came from, or who I was back home in Texas.

But there is a beautiful lesson I've learned in all of this. Whether I'm completely alone or feeling tormented by loneliness, in each case, the overriding truth is that God is *with* me. In fact, He's closer than that. *He's in me.*

So, as I sit alone in this dark cabin, deafened by the noise of silence, I am reminded that there is nothing to fear. I am never actually alone.

He is here. And wherever you are, alone or lonely, He is with you, too.

Chapter 12

Paradigm Shift

"Only God can fully satisfy the hungry heart of man." ~ Hugh Black

According to the New Oxford American Dictionary, a "paradigm shift" is *a fundamental change in approach or underlying assumptions.*

Picture this. You're harnessed into this strange contraption that resembles a giant backpack undergirded by a knot of seat belts that forms a makeshift chair. Behind you, a zany parachute pilot is attached to your back like a Siamese twin. You quickly realize that this guy is expecting you to abandon the comfort of solid ground in order to run down a steep mountain-slope, so that the wind can whisk you away into the expansive sky above you.

Your internal dialogue is all over the place. *Oh my gosh! What in the world am I doing? Am I going to plummet to my death? I feel so out of control! What if my harness breaks or what if the wind sweeps me up into the atmosphere forever? I feel so helpless! I hate not being in control!*

The next thing you know, your thoughts are interrupted, and you've miraculously found the courage to trot down the hill with a heavy parachute and pilot in-tow. Then, all of a sudden, the wind takes you away and you're floating high above the ground where your feet were just planted. Is it beautiful? Is it scary? Can you breathe?

After you catch your breath, you imagine yourself as a bird, soaring on the wind, thankful to see the world from such an awesome perspective two thousand feet above the earth! As you sit back, enjoying the view, you realize how peaceful it is to be so far from the world below. Life up high is inspiring and exciting, a little scary, and yet one of the most serene things you've ever experienced.

You begin to fully trust that the pilot knows what he's doing. The frenetic pace of fatalistic thoughts in your mind has now subsided. This is calm, quiet, soul-filling peace.

After you bask in this peace for a while, you decide to "kick it up a notch" by requesting some air-craziness. The pilot complies and you immediately start spiraling towards the ground below, and then rock back and forth like you're on a gigantic swing. *Whoopee! What fun!* Everything looks a blur, but the speed and the feeling of the loss of control is now thrilling and exhilarating. You don't want this moment to end, but it must. After numerous spins and flips and turns, you descend towards green ground. The pilot guides you in and asks you to place your feet on the green grass below. You do whatever he says, because as exciting as the flight was, that ground looks pretty hard.

The landing goes smoothly, and now you are squatted in the cool grass with a large parachute and pilot at your back, realizing that the ride is finished. Your twenty minutes of airtime exhilaration is over.

But the beautiful thing is this: you abandoned your need to be in control and you put your trust in the pilot, and now you're changed because of it. Life looks a little different. You feel refreshed and renewed because you have a new perspective on life and because you understand that things were never "out of control." They were only out of *your* control. The pilot knew what he was doing the whole time. Your job was to trust him and enjoy the ride, because in trusting you would experience things you never had before.

Life can be just like that. It can feel completely out of your control at times. You wonder why everything is spinning and blurry and moving full-speed ahead. You wonder when the fear, the anxiety, the heart palpitations will stop.

In August 2003, I felt like my life was spinning out of control. I was nestled snug in my twin bed, a light French breeze tickling my skin as I slept, when I was awakened by a faint knock on my bedroom door. I was a *jeune fille au pair* in France at the time. I was living with an American family that I had only worked for just three short weeks, and the quiet knock came from the dad, who was standing behind my bedroom door whispering, "Bethany, I hate to wake you, but your dad is on the phone. I think it's urgent."

With grogginess and a fluttering heart, I grabbed the phone from him and croaked in my best morning voice, "Hello?" In the moments that ensued, my dad proceeded to tell me that my cousin, Chase, had been killed in a car accident just a few hours before in my Texas hometown. Honestly I don't remember any other part of the conversation. I only remember that when I hung up the phone, I closed my eyes to the world around me and cradled myself into a ball, attempting to rock myself out of this nightmare.

After a few hours, I threw on my clothes, grabbed my bag and headed out to the local cheese market, hoping that the stench of moldy cheese delicacies would snuff-out the scent of heartache and heaviness that had so quickly become my companion. This stinky cheese Band-Aid worked until I went to reverse my car out of the market traffic and was rear-ended by my literal neighbor.

The pity party came to town, and I thought, *Could this day get any worse?*

Well, it did.

That night I decided to fill the empty hole in my heart by distracting myself with a movie. It was my first time to visit the cinema just across the border in Switzerland. I cried into my store-bought *tabouleh* through the entirety of *Pirates of the Caribbean: The Curse of the Black Pearl*, and then continued to stuff my emptiness with a bar of *Caillier* Swiss chocolate.

Once the movie finished, I headed out to the parking garage and couldn't remember where I had parked. After pacing the length of a basketball court over and over, I gave up, and plopped myself into a pile on the cold, cement ground.

The tears streamed down my face like the colors that bleed off of a melted M&M.

After my meltdown, I picked myself up and miraculously found my car. I am actually proclaiming this a miracle! Then I drove back to my house along the dark, lonely streets of a sleeping city.

My routine in the days that followed included a daily conversation with one or various family members, offering comfort and support across oceans, since I wasn't able to make it back for the funeral. After one of these conversations, I had to quickly run to the store to do the grocery shopping, but upon getting to the car outside, I realized that I had not so conveniently left my car keys on the second floor of the house.

I charged up the stairs like a bull and managed to drag the rubber of my boot sole on the final wooden stair. I tripped and flew across the hallway, dragging my knees across the carpet on the way down as I landed flat on my face.

That's when I digressed. I started pounding my fists and kicking my feet on the floor like a spoiled child desperate for a shiny toy on the shelf at Target. I screamed and cried, and yelled out loud, "I can't do this!"

My eyes were blood-shot and tear-stained, my heart and fists numb from the throbbing pain of discouragement. I dragged myself to my bed and lay lifeless in a heap. Then something changed. God whispered into the cracks of my dried-out heart. He said, "Bethany, you can turn your back on me because of this, or you can turn your face toward me. I'll walk this road with you as your friend if you let me. It may not feel like it now, but I have everything under control."

Thankfully, wisdom chimed-in and I chose the latter.

Up to that point, I would've described myself as a good Christian girl, one who had a deep and profound relationship with God, the Creator of the world, and with Jesus, His Son. I would have told you that I knew this God as friend and comforter, and that I knew His ways were mysterious, but right and good.

And yes, all these things would've been true. But isn't it amazing what changes *in* us when something around us changes? I knew what to say. I knew how to say it. But in all honesty, I had no idea that God could be my friend. And perhaps more importantly, that He *wanted* to be my friend. I didn't know that, as my friend, this tragedy in my family's life had not only broken our hearts, but His.

That day, as I lay in my bed, in a foreign land, I felt at home in the arms of God, my friend, for the first time ever. I knew that, despite the heartache, confusion, and loneliness I was experiencing, He was in control of all things – even *this*.

This was the big moment, the "paradigm shift" I needed in my life. I was invited to experience a new understanding of God. I was committing to an adventure with Him. At the time, I didn't know what doors that would open, or how that decision would deeply impact the geography of my future and my career path. I just knew that moment where God spoke His friendship over my life with the gentle reminder that He has it all under control was the moment where my life radically shifted. He redirected the course of my life completely through that heart-wrenching experience.

In fact, fourteen years later, I reflect on the terrible events during that time of my life and give credit to God for so boldly and unmistakably grabbing my attention and focusing it back on Him. I reflect on how He reminded me through so many people and circumstances that He was in control, and that He was making the most of a chaotic situation. Through that rollercoaster of emotions, He put me on a trajectory towards a deeper, more authentic, more intimate relationship with Him.

God is the pilot of my life. When it feels like everything is dangerously spiraling out of control and towards the hard ground, I find comfort in knowing that God is at the helm. He is the expert. He is reading the direction of the wind and calculating the speed of the wind shears. He's guiding the parachute. And because I trust Him completely with my life, knowing that He is in total control, my gaze and focus has shifted. My new paradigm is that He is always in control, and always will be.

CHAPTER 13

Swiss Cheese & Living Water

Jesus answered, "Everyone who drinks this water will be thirsty again, but whoever drinks the water I give them will never thirst. Indeed, the water I give them will become in them a spring of water welling up to eternal life."
~ *John 4:13-14 (NIV)*

There I stood with a Kelly green mountain as my backdrop, with the still warm residue of chocolate on my lips. I was utterly and completely lost. Okay – perhaps that's not the precise truth: I knew I was in the heart of Switzerland somewhere near the *Nestlé-Callier* Chocolate Factory that had, only moments ago, added inches to my waistline.

And because I suddenly smelled strong wafts of cheese in the air, I assumed I was close to my hoped-for destination of Gruyère – the home of delicious Gruyère Swiss cheese.

That's when I heard the heavy hooves of a local army of cattle clomping towards me. Their melon-sized cowbells rang a symphonic melody in my ears, but it wasn't the magical appearance of foreign cows that struck me. It was the sight of the soldiers that led them - two young men, in their early twenties, dressed in Cookie Monster blue trousers, accessorized with matching suspenders, giant mud boots and tiny hats.

Ooooh, I thought, *to be lost in the Swiss Alps, only to be rescued by handsome Swiss farmers. What fun?* So I batted my eyelashes and played the role of a *damsel in distress*, conjuring up the best and worst of my French vocabulary.

Pointing to my chicken-scratched map created for me by our friendly chocolate factory *femme*, I asked in broken French, "Where is this place – *La Fromagerie?*"

After a "maybe over there," I got distracted and made a random request, "Can I take your picture to capture this very Swiss experience?" The answer came in the form of a nodded, "Yes," accented by a shy smile and followed by instructions to wait a few moments.

I watched the farmers corral their cattle into the *châlet*, and then waited as they slid over to me on a dance floor of soggy mud. With a slight and embarrassed hesitation, they then positioned themselves directly in front of the breath-taking Alps so the photography session could start.

Only then did I repeat with a giggle in my tone, "This is *so* Swiss for me. *You* are so Swiss." This comment ignited laughter in my two models, and then the blonde one winked at me and said, "Actually, we're Polish."

Laughter is contagious. It's a good thing that humiliation is not because we all would've stood there in an awkward silence. Luckily that was not the case. The two Polish farmers quickly invited me to tour their mountainside barn, and despite my embarrassment, I embraced the adventure of this encounter and followed my new friends inside. Not only did I get a personal tour soaked in the stench of fresh cow manure, but I also learned that they, too, make Gruyère cheese. I put my camera to use again and smirked at the odds: *What are the chances of getting lost in the Alps and meeting Polish farmers who make Swiss cheese?*

I had been lost in the Swiss Alps. I thought I found what I was looking for, but it turns out I found something completely different standing in front of me.

Life is funny like that.

Because of all of my ministry work and travels around the world, I consider it one of the biggest blessings of my life to stay with people wherever I travel. Sometimes my hosts are already friends, but more often than not, they are strangers who quickly *become* friends over the duration of my stay with them.

I was in Scotland a few years ago, and my heart was deeply impacted by the generosity, eccentricity, and color of a couple I met there. I'll call them Maude and Bobby.

I flew into Edinburgh, and through jet-lagged eyes was looking to meet my hostess at the airport baggage claim. I searched high and low, and couldn't seem to find a match for the description I'd been given. Then out of nowhere, from behind me I heard a very thick, mumbled Scottish accent, "Bethany, Bethany! Is that you?"

I giggled to myself as I turned to face my hostess already aware that this was going to make for a good trip and an even better story.

Maude had flashy maroon hair and a small-frame body donning a green flower print skirt, hot pink top, and a blue tattered sweater. She was wearing white socks, which reached halfway up her calves and brown hiking sandals on her feet. We hugged like old friends and made our way to the car rental place so I could chauffeur us back to her home since she'd ridden the city bus to the airport.

Once in the car, Maude fired question after question to me about my life, travels, experience with Scotland, and pretty much every other category under the sun. I'm not sure I muttered more than two words before she was on to the next question. I had to aptly tune my ears for this verbal exchange because her accent was thick like wool, and she spoke at lightning speed.

We eventually pulled into her driveway, and as I got out of the car to unload my bag, a bubbly man bounced up to me, embracing me in a giant bear hug. Bobby is the friendliest Scot I've ever met.

I spent three nights at Maude and Bobby's home, and over time came to learn the ins and outs of each of their stories. One of my favorite moments was sitting with them at dinner feeling like my head was on a swivel. I kept turning from one to the other to listen to them talk because they kept telling me different stories at the same time. When I'd face Maude to focus on her words, Bobby would talk louder. When I'd face Bobby, Maude would increase her volume. And so this went for the entire dinner.

It's as if they were fighting to be seen and heard. That felt familiar to me. In the middle of my swivel-headed-ness, I wondered how many times each day I fought to be seen and heard. *Whose attention was I after? Who did I want to take notice?* I snapped back into listening and out of my thoughts when they began to talk about their stout reliance on Jesus to meet all of their needs. Maude was searching for deep community, having been ousted in the past for her eccentric ways and obsession with pinching pennies to save up to travel the world, but she leaned on Jesus. Bobby was full of joy, but had come from a rough life. In fact, his story really impacted me because he was hopelessly lost until he found Jesus when he was looking for something else.

Bobby had lived on the streets of Edinburgh for twelve years as a homeless alcoholic. He had been stabbed over five times while living on the streets. The last time Bobby was stabbed, he was admitted to the local hospital. During his recovery, he became restless, and escaped out the window in his hospital gown in search of a strong drink.

Desperation led him into a nearby church. Not wanting to interrupt the service, Bobby sat at the back on a pew, dozing on and off into sleep as he waited to approach church members for money. Something happened as he was waiting and dozing, though. His heart felt warm, his fingers felt tingly, and his mind was inexplicably clear. He heard the pastor sharing about something called "the gospel," and suddenly, all he could think about was Jesus. Tears streamed down Bobby's face, and he answered the call to follow Jesus in that very moment.

He went out onto the streets straight after that supernatural encounter and told every person he saw that he just met Jesus. Then when he decided to get baptized a few weeks later, Bobby walked into the local police station and invited the police chief to his baptism. He wanted him to see that he had really changed, and that he was not the criminal that the police had come to know so well. The police chief and some of the other policemen attended the baptism service, and the chief stood up and spoke the following words to those in the crowd: "I came here today because I couldn't believe Bobby's life change to be true. But if what he is confessing is real, all I can say is that all the police in Edinburgh will rest well tonight!"

After Bobby's baptism, he voluntarily turned himself in for all the crimes he had previously committed – breaking and entering, robbing liquor stores, and theft. He then stood before a judge to testify and Bobby said, "I stand here today as a man in relationship with God, who is even more powerful than you, sir." The judge was slightly taken aback, but said to Bobby, "I'm going to take a chance on you.

I'm giving you three months in prison, but if I ever see you before me again, I'll make sure it's three years behind bars." With that, Bobby did his time and to this day, nearly forty years later, he lives as a sold-out follower of Christ.

Bobby was lost. He thought he knew what he was looking for all those years. He chased after a drink to soothe his restless soul. Bobby found a drink, but it didn't look anything like what he expected. It wasn't in the form of beer, wine, or liquor. It was the Living Water of Jesus Christ – the unexpected drink that never runs dry.

I think about the story of Jesus where he engages the woman at the well and offers her the hope and sustenance of Living Water. Jesus peered into her soul, spoke truth to her about everything she'd ever done, and offered her the opportunity to never experience deep thirst again.

Just like Bobby, she didn't expect to meet Jesus when she did. She was chasing another kind of drink. And just like Bobby, she responded in faith. Just like Bobby, she ran out and told everyone she knew of this Living Water. And just like Bobby, her life was radically and eternally changed in one short moment.

I think about my life and yours in this regard. Am I lost? How am I searching? What is desperation driving me towards? What am I seeking? What am I thirsting? What well am I hanging out at hoping that it will fill my emptiness?

We're all searching for something. Whether it's reaching for another drink at the bar like Bobby, or searching for true community like Maude, or whether it's seeking love through a man like the woman at the well, we are all seeking. We're tired, we're thirsty, and whether we realize it or not, our souls are desperately craving even the smallest a splash of Living Water.

But Jesus is always right there. He's on the streets with us. He's in the hospital rooms. He's on the buses and in the subways. He's in the pews at the back of the church.

We can always find Him at the well - that place where we keep returning to in order to find our peace, security, and filling for the day. He's right there, and He's offering us an opportunity for more. He's inviting us to drink of Him, the Living Water that quenches our thirst forever and ever. And because of that, we are thankful that we've found more in Him than what we were looking for in anything else.

Jesus, my Living Water. Jesus, yours, too.

CHAPTER 14

Mountain Girl

"Soak me in your laundry and I'll come out clean, Scrub me and I'll have a snow-white life... God, make a fresh start in me, Shape a Genesis week from the chaos of my life." ~ *Psalm 51:7,10 (MSG)*

Becoming a "mountain girl" has never been my goal, mostly because it implies things that I simply don't understand – hiking boots, Swiss army knives, sleeping bags, tents, giant backpacks, dry food, and hard ground. These things aren't bad. They just aren't *me*.

While living in Switzerland, I found myself playing the role of "mountain girl" quite often though. One week in particular, I went with my mission staff on a team-building trip to the breath-taking Lauterbrunnen Valley. The weather was absolutely gorgeous and along with the scenery, both served as the perfect backdrop for our two-day hiking adventure.

After trekking across semi-flat terrain through the valley on our first afternoon, we made a steep ascent up to Gimmelwald, a picturesque mountain village, where we decided to warm ourselves with hot chocolate on the balcony of a local restaurant. Just as my mug reached my lips for the first time, I glanced sideways and saw a man with three goats in tow next to our table. There was an exchange of dialogue with a nearby local, and we soon learned that the goat man was asked by his friend in a higher-altitude mountain village to transport his three goats down the mountain for him. Every time the goat man arrived to a new village thinking it was his final destination, the locals would tell them he was in the wrong village. So off he went, with these three goats, looking for the right village over and over again. We giggled at this silly story because it sounded like the ultimate prank to us: "Here friend, take my three goats... forever!"

These mischievous goats made themselves at home sniffing our hot chocolate and chewing Edelweiss petals. A grey kitten appeared out of nowhere and helped itself to a woman's hot chocolate, too. Suddenly, this local Swiss village had turned into an animal farm. The perfect summary of our odd morning break was a sign in front of the restaurant that read in English, ironic because none of the staff spoke English: "Horse**** Balls."

That was only the beginning of an adventure-filled hiking trip.

We traveled further up the mountain and then it was time to "hit the hay," literally. We spent the night in a fully functioning barn on beds of straw, complete with the leftover odor of goats. It was difficult to breathe at first because the allergens and smells were overwhelming, but in normal fashion, I always travel with an eye mask. You never know when you need one to shield that little light that won't stop blinking loudly in the silence of the dark or to shield straw from climbing up your nose and out your eyeballs while you sleep in a goat barn.

To my surprise, the straw was comfy and warm, and I was miraculously able to breathe the next morning upon waking.

Our team continued up the mountain just after breakfast to soak in the stunning view of the Eiger, Monch, and Jungfrau peaks. For lunch, we made *Pasta Pronto* and indulged in some handpicked wild blueberries. We descended all the way down the luscious green path to Lauterbrunnen late that afternoon. We celebrated our two-day adventure with a pizza dinner in the tiny town of Wengen, and then settled in to the Valley Hostel for the night.

All was going as planned during this team-building outing, until I woke-up on my skinny, cold hostel bed in the middle of the night with terrible stomach pains. I'll save you the gory details, but just imagine that you're in a hard bed in a strange place and you can't keep anything down. The closest toilet is down two flights of stairs in a shared space. You're as white as a ghost, and you're with a group of people you just met. In fact, out of six people, you're one of two girls. You're a three-hour curvy-road van ride away from home. Are you feeling sick yet?

The plan was to finish our team-building adventure with a fun event on the way back to Geneva that Saturday morning, but needless to say, it was canceled on account of my horrid state of health. We piled in the van, and I took a bucket and a giant bottle of water with me to the front seat. I closed my eyes. I opened them. I closed my eyes. I opened them. Nothing seemed to help ease my nausea. Thankfully, we stopped halfway home for a pit stop.

European road trips aren't like American ones. There's not a fast food chain on every corner or roadside favorites like Cracker Barrel or Buc-ee's in Texas. Because they are so few and far between, the travel centers are like miniature malls, often in the middle of nowhere. They have restaurants with long buffet lines and various other food options – some formal with steaks and others casual like McDonald's.

As I stepped out of the van that day, my stomach took a turn for the worst. I had high hopes that all would be okay because in a few moments, I would make it safely to the toilet. I didn't anticipate that upon entering the travel center and turning the corner to face the long hallway resembling a "road that never ends," I would see a line for the women's restroom about twenty miles long. I breathed deeply and slowly, and painstakingly waddled to the end of the line. After what felt like hours of relentless waiting, I stumbled into a stall and made friends with the toilet. I'll spare you the details and the parts of this story that made it my most embarrassing moment *ever*, and just say that we eventually loaded back into the van to complete the longest three-hour road trip I've ever taken. When we finally made it to my house, I bolted inside, dove into my bed, and fell into a deep sleep for days. For seventy-two hours, I could hardly move and surfaced from my bed only for emergencies. My head was like a record on repeat, constantly spinning. My stomach was like a butter churn, agitated. I had never been so sick in my entire life.

During those hellacious days, I lived on a diet of toast, bananas, applesauce, and popsicles.

It was only days later, after my full recovery, that I had the energy to clean out my hiking gear. I pulled out my water bottle and went to scrub it in the sink. To my horror, I found a thick black mark on the inside of it and immediately began to wonder how someone could write so straight and small with a Sharpie marker on the inside of a water bottle. But as I began to scrub it off, I had a devastating realization. It wasn't permanent marker. It was black mold.

I was a victim of "black-mold-itis."

Let me tell you something, it's not an "itis" you ever want to have. In fact, to this day, I inspect every nook and cranny of a water bottle before using it.

Up to that point, I had assumed that I either had food poisoning from the pizza I had the night before my illness struck or from the cow-breath tainted water from the troughs we drank from during our hike.

Considering that our entire team ate the same food and drank the same water, I decided that black mold was the culprit. I had no idea that the thing I carried in my pack as my vessel for one of life's necessities — water - was the very thing that caused my downfall. The water was mountain fresh. My water bottle looked clear. The black mold was sneaky. It was hidden in the corner, nearly too small to detect, at the bottom of the bottle and took the shape of someone's initials written in permanent marker.

It is scary because when I was overheated, I drank from that bottle. When we had breakfast or lunch, I drank from that bottle. When I was tired, I drank from that bottle. When I was thirsty, I drank from that bottle. In the middle of the night when I woke up and couldn't sleep, I grasped for that bottle. It was within close reach at every single moment, and I relied on it to revive and refresh me. Little did I know, the unseen toxins inside were warring against my body.

I think about the things in my life right now that might be lurking in the crevices of the water bottles of my life. What am I running to for rehydration and replenishment? What do I keep within close reach to revive me? What am I looking for to fill my empty soul? What am I grasping at that is actually waging war against my body?

The danger is that, oftentimes we reach for these things, thinking they are good for us. They bring refreshment, revitalization, and rehydration. But there are vicious toxins lurking out of plain sight. There are things that are part of our daily routine that are wreaking havoc on our mental, spiritual, emotional, or physical lives.

I think of a particular toxic entanglement I had with a non-boyfriend over a period of nine years. On the surface things seemed fine. We were just friends. We only officially dated for a period of three months and didn't venture towards anything permanent beyond that. I remember him telling me in the early days to "not fall in love with him because he'd break my heart." I remember thinking that was stupid. *Of course, I wasn't going to fall in love with him.*

Three months somehow morphed into nine hot and cold years. He became like that water bottle for me. I reached for him around every corner and every turn. I reached for him to emotionally fill the empty spots in my heart and the missing pieces of my life. I leaned on him. I trusted him. I ran to him first for everything. Over time, it became an idolatrous obsession.

It took years for me to realize that the vessel I reached for – this guy – was toxic. He took me on an emotional rollercoaster ride for nearly a decade – never committing to me, and eventually breaking my heart into a thousand, jagged pieces. When I was with him, the water seemed clear. It seemed healthy. But there were toxins lurking below, hiding in the corners. And after spending so much time and investing so much into this guy, it wreaked havoc and hell on my life.

I tried several times to break away from this entanglement, but it was only years later, on the side of another Swiss mountain, that I desperately cried out to God to release me from the bondage of this relationship. Just like I drank the toxic water repeatedly on that hike, resulting in debilitating sickness for three days, this toxic relationship with this guy ended in a spiritual retching. For three days straight, I cried as the toxins of emotional abuse and idolatry came out of me like a dark flood. God was doing His beautiful work of healing. It was painful, cleansing, and life-saving.

Just like my body needed to detoxify from the mold I'd been consuming on our hike, my heart and mind needed the same.

I don't know about you but I know in my life that God has used hurt and pain to bring about His healing. I believe that to be true. Even when I was lying in bed in so much pain and sicker than I'd ever been, I knew that's what my body needed. My body needed to rid itself of the toxins I had ingested repeatedly. When my heart was battered and bruised from years of a non-committal toxic relationship, I knew that the pain had to be extracted before the true healing could begin.

I've learned that there is always purpose in the pain. God uses it to rid us of toxins, so that we can be refueled and refilled with His clean and clear Living Water. Allowing Him to extract those toxins is necessary for our healing.

And it's still a good idea to inspect your water bottles anyway.

CHAPTER 15

The Wildness of Aliveness

"I travel not to go anywhere, but to go. I travel for travel's sake. The great affair is to move." ~ Robert Louis Stevenson

One of my favorite things when I lived in Europe was that I could take a train almost anywhere. It didn't matter if I was jumping the local twenty-minute express line to the city of Geneva, or cashing in my ticket for a six-hour long journey to Venice, Italy. If I was on a train, it meant that I was going somewhere.

Despite being surrounded by people, it also meant that I had time alone. I had time with my thoughts and time to stare out the window mesmerized by the blurred and hazy mesh of greens and blues swirled together by the motion of a high-speed train. I had time to sit with my eyes glazed-over listening to the warm sounds of Sarah McLachlan.

Sarah McLachlan is one of my go-to artists. Her voice is soothing and familiar. Whenever I can't sleep on a long-haul overseas flight, I flick my playlist to Sarah. Whenever I'm feeling sad, lonely, or anxious, Sarah is one of the voices that silences my wandering thoughts. I can tune-in Sarah and shut out the world.

One of my biggest weaknesses is that I am always on the move, and if I'm not actually moving, I'm thinking about my next move.

I think back to my childhood, which was extremely stable. I lived in the same house from the time I was two to twenty-four. But, the "travel bug" bit me early. I came from a line of "travelers" – my dad's parents loved traveling and made a huge effort to see as much of the world as possible. My mom and dad have carried on that same legacy and continue to be fascinated by traveling the world.

Sitting on a Swiss mountainside one evening in a rare moment of stillness, blanketed by a beautiful autumn night sky, I was reminded that my heart beats for the "wildness of aliveness." While everything around me is quiet and calm, I am still running circles in my head to keep moving, to keep pace, to protect my own need for movement with the gift of remembrance.

I think about moments slurping hot chocolate in my favorite Parisian café just outside the *Centre Pompidou* as I watched the street artist contort his body, while flames spewed from his mouth.

I think about running down green hills, bursting with red poppies on a temperate spring afternoon in Switzerland.

I think about the taste of my favorite *Rooster Chianti,* perfectly complemented by a wedge of *Saint André* cheese spread onto a warm baguette, under a splattered sky of stars.

I think about lying on the cold concrete of a winding farm road, as I lay down between the grape vineyards to catch my breath from my homeward hike. I put my I-Pod music on shuffle, in hopes that God would whisper something profound into the corners of my heart. I smirk when I think that many times the same song repeatedly ministered to me: *Fix You* by Coldplay.

I think about swinging my legs atop a ski lift, pondering the bliss and blessing of a life where snowboarding with international *au pairs* was a part of my job.

I think about lunches on the Coppet Dock of Lake Geneva, where *La Vache Qui Rit* cheese with sun-dried tomatoes and San Pellegrino water were staples.

I think about walking my favorite dog, Ollie, around the neighborhood under the bizarre glow of guacamole moonlight, thankful that things aren't always as they seem and similarly grateful that God gives us the creativity and imagination to believe that things can always be *more* than they seem. A normal night stroll can quickly turn into a fairytale when the moon looks like guacamole. That mild green glow reminds me of the warmth, friendship, and love around an evening meal of salsa, chips, and homemade guacamole.

These sweet memories cling to me like leggings on a hot day. I am thankful for the "wildness of aliveness," that which is the ability to think, remember, and ponder the days that have been the building blocks of my life.

It's so easy to live inside your head and forget that there is a world going on around you, a world that, despite your temporary immobility, is constantly moving.

Jesus was the master of the "wildness of aliveness." He was always moving or thinking about His next move. Beyond that, when Jesus moved toward people in love, He brought radical transformation to their lives.

He healed lepers. He gave sight to the blind. He valued women. He engaged with foreigners. He fought for justice. He breathed peace. He raised people from the dead.

What was wild about Him? Everything. For starters, He was God in the flesh. He gave up a life in heaven, the most beautiful, ethereal place our human minds can't even begin to conceive. He turned His back on that for this world, for the broken and waywardness of a human-tainted earth.

Jesus was wild everywhere he went. He was wild in conversation. He was wild in belief. He was wild in rebelling against culture, religion, and things that held people in bondage. The way He lived and moved on this earth, every tiny thing about Him, was wild.

I think about the story where, for two days, Jesus intentionally delayed going to the deathbed of his friend, Lazarus. Mary, Martha, and Lazarus were some of his closest friends, and he wasn't in any hurry. That's wild!

In that wildness of doing things differently than what people expected, it gave opportunity for Jesus to raise Lazarus from stale death. Lazarus hadn't just taken his last breath; he had been dead for three whole days. His body reeked and decay had already set in. But just in that moment of total hopelessness, Jesus stepped in and did the wildest thing He could. He called Lazarus out of the grave and back to life.

Here's the crazy thing. Jesus was always on the move, but not at the expense of *seeing* people as he went. He was on the move *looking* for people.

As I travel I want that to be my focus: looking for people, seeing them exactly where they are. I want to look for smiles and for broken hearts. I want to look for moments to connect in the big things and in the small things. I want to look because I'm fascinated by the stories of intertwining lives. I want to look because there's purpose on the path of every person we cross. I want to look because Jesus looked and He *saw*. I see because He has given me His eyes to see.

Do I always see perfectly or look upon others with a clear gaze? No. In fact, I often falter in this. But when I intentionally open my eyes to see people where they really are, God always shows up.

I traveled to Curitiba, Brazil in the summer of 2014 to lead a short-term mission project. As I was preparing to train and lead sixty-five volunteers, God kept pressing on my heart to ask Him to give me "eyes to see as He sees." This was my prayer throughout the trip, and a constant challenge to our mission teams during our time in Brazil.

In fact, I was in the habit of waking up every morning asking the simple question: "God, what do *You* want me to see today?" He answered that vividly each day, whether it was looking into the eyes of a child living in poverty as I was washed her feet, or whether it was through a conversation with one of the local pastors about his heart to see the gospel transform his community. God showed up every time I opened my eyes.

One encounter stands out above all the rest, though. We were visiting a homeless population in the *Passeio du Publico* one Sunday morning and gathered under a gazebo in the pouring rain to sing *My Redeemer Lives* in Portuguese and English. After that, we sang a Brazilian song about the power and comfort of God's embrace. While the worship leader sang the song, the local volunteers, along with our mission team, walked around the large gazebo touching people on the shoulders, hugging them, and laying hands on their heads in prayer. After this time, the pastor invited our mission team to pray with the homeless men and women in attendance.

Everything in me locked up in that moment. Fear overtook. I didn't know the language and I didn't know these people, so how could *I* pray with them?

I don't know if you've ever had an experience like this, but when

God asks me to do something, which feels wildly out of my comfort zone, my body usually tenses up and the arguments in my head start popping-off like firecrackers at a Fourth of July celebration. Every single reason I can't do something fills my head. Every reason I'm unworthy, incapable, or ill equipped starts to flood my heart and mind.

My self-talk gets really grim in those moments. The words I spew into my own heart are degrading and abusive. But when I step away from those ugly thoughts and silence my mind, I can always hear the whisper of Jesus: *I've chosen you for this moment.*

When God gives you an assignment, oftentimes it makes very little logical sense. But that's the whole point – He chooses us to walk out our *faith*, not our sight. Yet, he surprises us because in so doing, He generously gives us the ability to see as He sees.

I would like to tell you that my obedience that day was instantaneous. I'd like to tell you my words were brave and bold like Moses', "Here am I, send me," but the truth of the matter is that pride delayed my decision to obey God. I was leading the team, and pride snickered at me, "You can't ask your team to pray with these people if you don't have the bravery and boldness to do it yourself."

I blocked the voice of doubt and stepped out in bravery. I immediately found myself face-to-face with Julienne and Jaime, a young couple who were sitting at a table eating the sandwiches they had just been handed by some of our other volunteers. With the help of my interpreter, Ana-Paolo, I asked them if they wanted prayer. Their response was hesitant, but desperate, "We want to be released from the bondage of cocaine so that we can be there for our three children." I learned more about their family dynamic – they had three children together, but weren't married and spent every weekend on the streets getting high. Tears filled my eyes. I knew that God was stirring in my heart with His.

So I began to pray out loud over this young couple, and as I did, Ana-Paolo interpreted each line. It was a slow and frustrating process, and I felt a sharp sense of urgency. I knew God wanted to do more in this moment for Julienne and Jaime than translate my words from English to Portuguese.

In a moment of bravery I stopped my prayer, and dug into my

satchel bag, pulling out a small bottle of peppermint oil. I then asked Julienne and Jaime separately if I could anoint them and pray for them again. They simultaneously nodded, "Yes."

I told them that whenever they smelled or tasted peppermint flavor in the future that it would be a reminder of this moment, and more importantly, a reminder that God is always with them.

I faced Julienne. I knelt down in front of her, doused my fingers in peppermint oil, and drew an oily cross on her forehead. I then placed my hand on her head and began to pray, empowered by the Holy Spirit. As I was praying that God would release her from the bondage of drugs and by Christ's authority that she would be declared "free," I saw a white light enveloping her, washing out the darkness, and replacing it with hope. I began weeping for her, not out of a place of empathy, but out of a deep spiritual understanding of how God sees her and loves her. I finished praying, stood to hug her, and when I did, she began sobbing and shaking. I believe God was literally freeing her from the chains of bondage in that very moment.

I then turned to Jaime, a strong and staunch man, and anointed him with peppermint oil. As I was praying, I told him I felt God was calling him out to be the leader of his family. I told him that I saw arrows flying at his back, but that Jesus was wrapping himself around him so that the arrows couldn't touch him. I told him that God was breaking the shell of the old person that he was and was calling him forward to be the man God created him to be. The more I said, the faster the tears fell from his eyes. Again, I believe God was doing the incredible work in that very moment of releasing this man from the yoke of bondage that had held him captive for so long.

After my encounter with Julienne and Jaime, I was headed to the other side of the gazebo to meet with our team. As I was walking, I saw a dark, stoic figure leaning against a pole. He was a young man, wearing all black, which mirrored the circles under his eyes. I paused in front of him.

"Can I pray for you?"

He gave me a sideways glance, rolled his eyes, and muttered, "*Sim*" (yes). He then said in broken English, "My name is Alan."

I pulled the peppermint oil out of my pocket and told him the same thing I had said to Julienne and Jaime, "When you smell or taste peppermint, let it be a reminder of this moment and that God is always with you."

He nodded in agreement. I anointed him, placed my hand on his forehead, and then began to pray over him.

He stared coldly at me while I prayed. I didn't care, though, because I knew God wanted to say something to Alan, and I wasn't going to leave until He did.

Just a few minutes into my prayer, the Holy Spirit began downloading so much into my heart for this man standing before me. I stopped, and looked straight into Alan's eyes. He looked away, but I began to speak anyway.

I said, "God wants you to know that you are not a failure. He loves you. He sees you." Alan turned to face me at this point, his tear-filled eyes now locking with mine.

I continued, "He knows your pain. When you think you are alone, He is there. When you think no one understands, He does. Trust Him. He loves you more than you know."

I then asked him if I could hug him. He nodded in permission. I latched onto him, and he began to weep. The dam of pain and torment, doubt and failure, forcefully broke in that moment. The tears flowed freely and unendingly. Alan's body shook, and he gripped me tight for three minutes straight. This grown, previously stoic man wouldn't let get of me. In that moment I was the arms of Jesus, and God was at work healing, restoring, and filling Alan's emptiness with His deep, ceaseless love.

After praying that day with Julienne, Jaime, and Alan, I was broken. I was broken because God had given me His eyes to see, and more importantly, to love. I was changed because His love flowed through me like a vessel to transform lives. It wasn't my power; it was His.

God was so gracious. He gave me His eyes to see people exactly where they were. He gave me eyes to see how He saw them, and the bravery to act on sharing that with them.

I think back to my craving to constantly be on the move. I think about the wildness of aliveness, and the way Jesus demonstrated wild, unwavering faith. He did this through seeing people with His Father's eyes.

I want to be wild like Jesus. I want to move toward people and have eyes to always see them as God sees them.

Chapter 16

Frozen Exasperation

*"God is our shelter and our strength. When troubles seem near,
God is nearer, and He's ready to help. So why run and hide?"*
~ Psalm 46:1 (The VOICE)

I've lived in a lot of places, but when it comes to filling my plate full of adventure, nowhere compares to Switzerland. It's a country where the motto might as well be, "Work Hard, Play Harder." It didn't matter the season of the year; every weekend hosted a new adventure for my friends and me.

The winter adventures generally revolved around snow, mountains, and adrenaline rushes. One of my favorite activities is, what I like to call, "extreme sledding."

Let me invite you to picture this for yourself.

You're all bundled-up like an over-stuffed Cabbage Patch doll, complete with hat, goggles, neck gator, mittens, and layers upon layers to keep you warm. You're seated twelve inches above the ground on a hard, wooden, ribbed sled with your legs sprawled apart in front of you. You're wearing sturdy ankle-supporting boots because they will serve as your only set of brakes, and you're clinging tightly to a frayed rope that will be your "lifeline" for the next thirty minutes of this thrill-ride down the mountain.

This extreme sledding, a bit like riding a bucking bronco, is no *mamsy-pamsy* thing. You board your sled and hold on for dear life because you'll be speeding down a three-mile sled run that winds through thick forest and intersects with ski runs throughout the course of the trail. Imagine yourself riding rough ocean waters on a Wave runner. Now put yourself on thick snow, with steep declines and moguls around every corner, with people shooting in front, behind, and beside you on skis and snowboards. You hit speeds of twenty miles an hour, and always win the prize of frozen tears stuck to your cheeks by the time you reach the bottom of the slope.

Though not as radical, snowboarding comes in a close second to extreme sledding.

I worked with international high school students in Switzerland and one of them said to me once, "You're a snowboarder, aren't you? You totally look like one." I took that as a compliment, so I decided to *become* one. Although, truth be told, it's a minor miracle that I still love snowboarding because I had a rocky start when I was first learning.

Right after I had taken up snowboarding, our Youth for Christ ministry staff went to the Alps for a retreat weekend. The chaotic morning we experienced getting to the retreat set the pace for the rest of the day. We arrived late at the train station parking lot, but like a kid running late for school, I tried to make up the lost time by sprinting without my shoes on. My bright turquoise ski socks were covered in gravel by the time we got to the train platform and my feet were aching, but even worse, we missed the train by a mere thirty seconds because Swiss trains are *always* prompt. We were able to catch the next train one hour later, though, and arrived to our mountain destination, *Les Diablerets,* later that afternoon.

We decided to make up for lost time and hit the slopes immediately. My friend, Jenna, and I walked half a mile from our cabin with our snowboards to the ski station and ascended the mountain on a lift. Once at the top, we boarded down the easy run at a novice pace. We were doing just fine until we realized the only way back up the mountain was to take the dreaded t-bar lift.

Switzerland has various types of ski lifts. First, there's the normal chair lift where you sit comfortably with one to three other people. Then, there is the butt-disc lift, where you balance your backside on this little button-thingy and proceed to let it pull you up the mountain, all the while hoping that you'll make it to the top without biting it or losing an important appendage. Lastly, there is the dreaded t-bar lift, where a bar-like contraption goes between your legs, like you're straddling a fence, while you hold a large skinny handle that pulls you forward up the mountain with a friend or stranger by your side.

The t-bar is the worst by far. And *yay*, that's exactly the type of lift that was looming in our very near future.

As new fans of snowboarding, Jenna and I looked at each other with wide eyes and raised eyebrows. We were barely able to even balance on our snowboards, let alone attempt a t-bar lift, which required excellent in-sync balance. We decided it was in the best interest to ride the lift solo.

Our first attempts were completely unsuccessful. When I bit it about one-eighth of the way up the slope in front of Jenna, I waited on her to pass by and decided to try to jump on her bar. Bad idea! We immediately fell over and Jenna shrieked because she thought she pulled her shoulder out of socket. *Oops*.

After recovering and laughing in pain like we'd just hit our funny bones, we gathered ourselves over at the side of the lift track and strapped on our boards, sliding down the mountain like injured puppies, headed for our second attempt at the infamous t-bar lift. This time, we thought we would ride up together, hoping we could help each other balance. Well, to our shock and delight, we made it on the first try and were doing really well balancing until, after giggling up a storm, I boasted, "This circus-act of us balancing on this stupid contraption would make a great America's Funniest Home Videos clip."

Pride comes before the fall. *Always*.

Not two seconds later, as we were approaching the halfway point of the lift: *CRASH! BANG! BOOM!*

I had hit a small bump, which threw us both off-kilter and then our boards simultaneously caught an edge, plummeting us to the ground like dominoes. Jenna managed to disconnect from the t-bar upon falling. I, on the other hand, did *not*.

I was still attached to the lift, not by my hands, but in-between my legs. I was being drug sideways up the steep slope of the mountain, hanging from the t-bar like a limp noodle. *Everything was upside-down*, and I was stuck in a very awkward and painful position.

I figured I had a few options in that moment. I could suck it up, pretend I wasn't in pain, and try to enjoy this unconventional upside-down ride up the mountain as much as possible, hanging on for dear life until I reached the top, or I could wiggle myself out of my attachment to the t-bar and then eventually hobble up the mountain, dragging my snowboard behind me.

I didn't have to decide. When my body hit another bump, my limp-noodle-self came unstuck. My legs crashed to the ground and I rolled five feet down the mountain like a giant snowball. When I stopped, I realized my knee was contorted in a way I didn't realize was possible, and unfortunately, I also noticed that I was in the direct path of the person behind me on the t-bar. I grunted and army-crawled to what felt like my death on the side of the lift track, and lay there in frozen exasperation. My cheeks were drenched from the kind of surface laughter that shadows misery and pain, and every muscle in my body felt like a wrung-out dishtowel.

As I lay there in a heap, snow piled under my neck like a firm pillow, I thought this might be my final resting place. It was beautiful here. The ice and snow would eventually numb my pain, and I would gently fall asleep into eternity.

I was jolted from my morbid thoughts when Jenna shouted my name from the top of the lift.

"Bethany! Are you alive?"

"Ugh," I grunted loud enough for her to hear thirty yards away.

"Do you need help? I can come down and get you."

"No, I'm okay. I'll be right up."

Twenty-four minutes later, I was reunited with Jenna at the top of the mountain.

It took all the energy I had to pick myself up out of the snow mass, collect what was left of my broken pride, and climb to the top of the mountain dragging my board behind me. I was mortified that I was in so much pain from a tortuous t-bar lift.

At the end of the day, my pride was shattered, I was slightly humiliated, and definitely in pain, but what mattered most is not that a t-bar had held me captive. It wasn't that blue and purple bruises became the new "black" on my body, or that I waddled in pain for days after the incident. What mattered most is that I picked myself up and carried my board to the top of that mountain.

It's so easy to "throw in the towel" when things don't go our way. It's easy to become melodramatic about the simplest of things.

Two days ago, one of my friends texted me about how enraged she was that her favorite breakfast stop was out of chocolate chip bagels. She told me she threw a small fit to the cashier and stomped out of the shop.

I didn't judge her. I didn't scold her. I just laughed, and then empathized with her.

How many times have I done that? The smallest of things hasn't gone my way, and it has knocked me completely off my rocker.

One summer when I was home from Europe, I was driving with my mom in her quiet residential neighborhood. I was going the speed limit, and a lady behind me in a mini-van sped up and started tailgating me. She then swerved to the left, into the opposite lane, and sped up to pass me. This was illegal. I looked over, and I have no idea what overtook me in that moment, but I put my pedal to the metal and glared out my driver's side window into her panicked eyes. I looked ahead, and in the opposite lane, where she was keeping pace with me like a NASCAR driver, a car approached. I didn't want to cause a wreck – I just wanted to make a point – so in a split second, I slammed on my brakes, and the lady veered safely back into the right lane directly in front of me. *Whew, we were safe.*

After my temporary moment of insanity, I slowly turned the corner and pulled up in front of my mom's house. She turned in her seat, looking me in the eyes, and demanded, "What is wrong with you? You could've killed all of us!"

I remember just sitting there, frozen. I felt numb. I felt exasperated. I felt like I couldn't move. I seriously had no idea what had just overtaken me, but I knew it was ugly.

Maybe I'd watched too many James Bond movies, maybe I thought I was invincible, or maybe I was just having a bad day. What I know to be true, though, is that I let the smallest thing – an annoyance about an impatient mini-van driver – rattle me to my core. My behavior was inexcusable, and my actions were completely unpredictable. That scared me. I had uncorked a side of myself I didn't even know was there.

I think back to my incident on the t-bar. I remember feeling numb. The world was literally upside-down at one point, and perhaps, sometimes, that's exactly how we feel - numb and upside-down. We are walking through this life, having just been drug sideways up a mountain or having been drug through an ugly marriage. Sometimes we've been drug through the throes of sleepless, selfless parenting for the first time or through the excruciating pain of the loss of spouse or best friend.

It is natural to feel numb and upside-down at times, but the important thing is that we remember that there are people who love and care for us. My friend, Jenna, was screaming out of concern for me from the top of that mountain. My mom knew the real me, and was deeply concerned about the non-Bethany-like actions that I had displayed during my road rage.

And just as importantly, these people help us pick ourselves up out of the heap of snow or help us out of our unpredictable rage. They talk us up. They talk us down.

When I think of the Holy Spirit at work in my life, He does that every day. He talks me up and He talks me down. In those unpredictable, painful, life-numbing moments, my self-talk can be downright ugly. I imagine yours is the same.

I beat myself up. I convince myself it's all over. I feel like a failure. I feel like a jerk. Shame overtakes me. Embarrassment overwhelms me.

I was leading worship at a women's conference a few months ago. It wasn't your typical polished, glossy event. It was a little bit messy, unpredictable, and raw. I've been to a lot of women's gatherings, and something I've noticed is that it's hard for us to be real and vulnerable with one other. Our default is to perfect our makeup, smile and say, "Everything's just great!"

This women's conference was so different. It was refreshing to hear the main speakers pouring their hearts out about the hard things in their lives and on their faith journeys. There were lots of tears among strangers, who now are friends because vulnerability connected us.

I was particularly struck by a message from one of the speakers. She talked about how, after teaching hundreds of women at a conference, a deep sense of insecurity overtook her, so much so, that she sat motionless in a pool of tears on her hotel room floor after giving her talk at the event. She vented to her husband over the phone and begged him to fly her home because she couldn't face anyone anymore with the sense of unworthiness she felt in her own life.

That resounded in my heart and mind for days after hearing her message. Watching her teach in front of thousands of women around the globe was a testimony to the fact that we are all there. We are all broken. The story doesn't end there, though, because, God uses our vulnerability to bless and encourage others.

Her story struck a chord with me because it was *my* story that weekend. I led worship from a broken heart. After two and a half years, my boyfriend and I had called it quits just days before. I was weak. I was an emotional wreck, and yet God asked me to use that in my leading. It's not what I wanted to do. I really wanted to cower in the corner and hide. But I led because it is what He asked me to do.

The day after that amazing conference, I wrote the following in my journal:

That sermon of raw confession and unworthiness shook me. I've wept in spurts about the very same thing – feeling so full, and yet so quickly emptied. Feeling so unworthy, broken, and messy – why would God use me? Why would He choose me? Why would He give me a voice? My heart has been shattered into a million pieces and I fight the battle daily that I am a failure. I have failed to do and be all that people want me to do and be. I'm not like them and never have been.

It's amazing how we can so easily forget that the people that love us are actually *for* us, and that more than that, *God is for us.*

I think back to my t-bar incident, to my road rage, to my friend and her chocolate chip bagel and to my broken heart exposed on a stage. We are real people who experience real pain and raw emotions. Sometimes that's ugly. Sometime's it messy. Sometimes we're broken.

But here's what I know. We are human, but God loves us anyway. And he does more than that. He takes our weaknesses and exchanges them for His strength. He gives us friends that call our name from the top of the mountain because they care. He calls us out of our frozen exasperation and gives us strength to pick up our snowboard and walk back up the mountain.

Chapter 17

Jump

"There is no fear in love. But perfect love drives out fear." ~ I John 4:18 (NIV)

In May of 2006, I was in Interlaken, Switzerland hosting sixty international au pairs on an adventurous weekend away. I had been on this same trip two times before with the ministry I worked for, and with each new trip came an itch to try another adrenaline-pumping activity. First it was paragliding, then it was white-water rafting, and this time, it was canyoning.

Canyoning can be described as a sport where one explores a canyon through various means: rappelling, rafting, floating, scaling cliffs, and waterfall jumping. And yes, it *is* as extreme as it sounds.

That chilly May afternoon, I managed with great difficulty to force my feet into the cold, soggy water boots and the black wetsuit that accompanied my bright yellow helmet and life vest. Fifteen of my fellow adventurers and I then squeezed into a van like sardines for the short ride up a nearby mountain. We unloaded like a parade of circus clowns when we reached the summit, and began to tromp through freezing cold water, tip-toeing across the jagged rocks beneath our feet.

At the end of this trek, as we arrived at the mouth of the canyon, our guide gave us some safety pointers for surviving this adventure. She said something that stuck with me for the rest of the day, "Once you start this journey, you cannot go back!"

Those words reverberated like cymbals crashing in my ears. Although I was nervous, I trusted the guide completely. So, onward I went turning every seed of doubt into great expectation for a thrilling day ahead!

The adventure began by repelling twenty-five feet down the side of a canyon wall, where my feet slipped a couple of times on the slick smooth rock face. After dangling in the air for a while, I managed to plop safely into a pool of swirling water. After that, along with my fellow canyoning crew, I climbed giant boulders, jumped into pools of water, and back-flipped off a few rocks here and there, letting the current gently take us down the mountain.

For the most part everything was relatively easy, and yet I felt a great sense of accomplishment. As soon as I had the hang of this canyoning thing, though, everything changed.

We climbed up what seemed to be just another giant boulder. But once atop the boulder, I looked out and felt a strong breeze from the wind tunnel, carved by the canyon walls. I realized I was now forty feet above the canyon river, and the only way down the mountain was to jump into the angry pool of swirling water taunting me below.

In that moment, despite all I had just accomplished and come through, fear consumed me.

My knees locked. I couldn't move. I couldn't breathe. All I wanted to do was to scale back up the canyon I had just descended. I've never prayed so fervently for the ability to fly in all of my life.

As I stood there in a state of panic, watching the others before me careen off the boulder to their certain death below, I remembered the words of the guide: "Once you start this journey, you cannot go back!"

I had no choice. Allowing fear to paralyze me atop that mountainous bolder was *not* an option. I had to risk. I had to jump.

Even though I'd never been in this exact situation before, my heart knew the all-to-familiar feeling of fear. Fear is a strange, powerful thing at times. Sometimes it triggers in me a desire to run away screaming from whatever it is that is scaring me. Other times, it pushes me into this weird, reclusive isolation or makes me want to give up altogether and throw in the towel.

Balancing on this giant rock, overlooking the rushing river of water below, I was feeling an overwhelming combination of all three!

I've always loved the story of Elijah, the Old Testament prophet, found in 1 Kings 19. The gist of the story is that God had just performed a miracle in front of the people of Israel. The prophets of Baal had built an altar, begging their god to consume it with fire and there was no answer, just silence. Nothing happened. Then Elijah built an altar, which he drenched with buckets of water, and after he prayed, fire fell from heaven and consumed it completely. The people of Israel praised God and then Elijah commanded them to seize the prophets of Baal. They did and killed every single one, 450 in total.

In the scene directly following this victory, the king at the time, Ahab, told his queen, Jezebel, all that Elijah had done and how he killed the prophets of Baal. Jezebel's responded by threatening Elijah's life.

Considering that Elijah had just witnessed a miracle, which resulted in victory for God and the Israelites, one would think he might have a chilled-out approach to this threat like, "Whatever, Jezebel. My God is bigger than your bad attitude threat."

Oh, but no.

Elijah panicked. In fact, Scripture clearly defines this, *"Elijah was afraid and ran for his life."* (1 Kings 19:3) And then, the drama escalates. Elijah travels with his servant and then leaves him to flee into the wilderness alone, where he asks God to take his life. *"I have had enough, Lord,"* he said. *"Take my life; I am no better than my ancestors." Then he lay down under the tree and fell asleep."* (1 Kings 19:4) Essentially, he wants to throw in the towel.

Fear is an odd thing, and we are susceptible to its power over us unless we act against it in faith. Fear is ultimately a *faith* issue. My paralysis atop that boulder exposed this in my heart. Where's my faith? Where's my trust?

We all struggle with the fear of something. For me, sometimes it's the fear standing on a boulder, seeing life flash before my eyes if I take one misstep. Sometimes it's the fear of sitting in my garage apartment staring out at the green sky, praying a tornado doesn't appear. Sometimes it's the fear of saying goodbye to people that I love around the world, not certain when I'll see them again. Sometimes it's the fear that I'll never amount to what God has called me to be. Sometimes it's the fear that I'll live my life selfishly and in vain. Sometimes it's the fear that I'll never be married or have a family of my own.

Whatever that fear may be in your own life, I know it's real and I know it can stop you in your tracks. But I also know this: I've had moments of paralyzing fear before, and I've experienced victory. I have moved overseas on my own. I have traveled across countries and cities by myself. I have left everything I've known to risk what might lay ahead. And in all these situations, God was with me every single time. He never left my side.

I had traveled down this canyon with Him, and now, standing on top of this boulder, He was still there right beside me. I wasn't going to give in and let fear stop me from what I had come to do. I was going to complete the journey before me, which required jumping into that rushing river with the faith that God would be with me!

The story of Elijah brings encouragement; God is with us when we are fearful. After Elijah wanted to throw in the towel, he laid down and fell asleep. Then, 1 Kings 19:5 says, "*All at once an angel touched him.*" God counteracted Elijah's fear with His nearness.

We see this in the life of Jesus as well. It is the crux of the gospel - Jesus came to touch humanity with His divinity.

God also sends his sustenance to Elijah. 1 Kings 19:5 continues with, "*All at once an angel touched him and said, 'Get up and eat.' He looked around, and there by his head was some bread baked over hot coals, and a jar of water. He ate and drank and then lay down again.*"

Can you imagine being awoken in a desert to the smell of warm bread? You've run from fear into isolation, and God provides you with the bread of His communion. It's an invitation to come and commune with Him.

He sees us, as we are, where we are. Even in our isolation. He reaches into the depth of our need and feeds us. He provides. He sustains. He takes care of us.

1 Kings 19:7 says, "*The angel of the Lord came back a second time and touched him and said, 'Get up and eat, for the journey is too much for you.' So he got up and ate and drank.*"

This strikes me. The angel comes back a second time. Why isn't once enough? I believe that it's because sometimes we need God's ministry repeatedly before we can understand the provision He is bringing us, the purpose to which He is strengthening us. Our humanity takes over and we want to push the snooze button on life at times, and turn our faces away from divine intervention because sleeping off that fear, that boulder before us, is easier.

But God is always sustaining and strengthening us for a purpose beyond what we can see. This is where our faith and trust comes in. God provides what we need exactly when we need it and most often, when we don't even know we need it. That's the *manna* in our life, which in the original Hebrew literally means, "What is it?"

God is on top of it. He knows what we need before we do.

That day, standing on that slippery boulder, pondering the chasm below, I wanted to run back up the mountain or hide in a crevice until it all just went away. All of these options seemed easier than jumping forty feet into a freezing mountain river to my possible death below.

But again, I didn't really have a choice. I had come all this way, up and down boulders, in and out of cold mountain water. I had to jump. So... with a renewed *umph* in my spirit, I stepped to the edge of the boulder and jumped! It was the most thrilling jump of my life, though not one I'd like to repeat!

That's the thing about our adventure of faith - once you start the journey of God, He loves you too much to let you give up. He always navigates us back to faith in Him. *"Strengthened by that food, Elijah traveled forty days and forty nights until he reached Horeb, the mountain of God."* (1 Kings 9:8b)

Through His nearness and touch, through His sustenance and provision, we are strengthened as He leads us back to the source of our faith and trust: Him.

Fear takes us away from God, but His perfect love casts out all fear. 1 John 4:18 says: *"There is no fear in love. But perfect love drives out fear."*

God is gracious; He navigates us back to Him. I think about Horeb, which is also called Mount Sinai. This was the sacred mountain of God where Moses met with God, and a place that represented the history and source of Elijah's faith. That's exactly where God led him.

What is the "mountain of God" in your life? Maybe it's a season of life where God provided for you in ways you didn't expect, or a relationship that always points you back to faith in Him. Maybe it's an event that happened, where you just *know* it was the hand of God leading you or a time when God surprised you with a job promotion or the restoration of a friendship.

I believe for you that beyond your fear, there is great faith. I believe that beyond fear, your "mountain of God" is awaiting to remind you of His faithfulness, provision, and perfect love in your life.

My prayer for all of us is that we open our hearts to let God draw us back in and restore us back to a place where our faith overtakes every fear.

CHAPTER 18

Lingering Presence

"Forever is composed of nows." ~ *Emily Dickinson*

When I worked in Switzerland, I lived with an American ex-pat family at *The Goat Farm*, a name derived from the direct translation of their street name, *Chemin de la Chevrerie*. The Bentzens lived in a spacious home and had made Geneva their home twenty-five years before. This was no ordinary family. They won my heart with unconditional love and wooed me into their family through gourmet dinner parties and late-night kitchen chats.

The Bentzens became my family during that season of life, especially since my own amazing family was 5,182 miles away. They called me their "Texas Blonde," and I took up residence in their home for three years.

Sharon Bentzen was a top-notch cook. As a young girl, I refused to let my mom teach me to cook because I didn't think I should have to learn *just because* I was a girl. Even though she excelled in the kitchen, I wanted nothing to do with prepping food because I would rather spend my days outside painting the sidewalk, writing in my journal, cuddling the cat, or assembling a new outfit for school. My kitchen rebellion resulted in the fact that I have two brothers that are fabulous chefs, leaving me, the non-chef, to fend for myself via Kraft macaroni dinners and quesadillas. I do make an excellent homemade salsa, and I admit that I stole the recipe from my older brother. While living in Switzerland though, I gained a new appreciation for the art of cooking. Sharon, the only American member of the prestigious Swiss cooking society, *Les Gourmettes,* shared some of her kitchen secrets with me.

Like my own mother, Sharon is an artist with a quirky flair for colors and bold tastes. After a long day at the ministry office, I would walk into the house, lulled by the aroma of simmering garlic and onions. I would offer my help, and it became pattern that I would either wash the mushrooms with a lemon-sized brush that resembled a mushroom, or I would chop vegetables. I enjoyed both jobs equally, because they were mindless and simple, and I really loved our deep chats in the kitchen while we were scrubbing, chopping, and simmering away.

I also thought I was a night owl until I met Sharon. I was warned the December before I moved into her home that "the Bentzens do *not* sleep." This thrilled me, actually. I've never been an early morning riser, mostly because my creative juices flow better after daylight hours and it was quickly apparent that this, too, was the way the Bentzens operated. I would return home after a late night out with au pairs and friends, and find Sharon whittling away at her latest creation in the kitchen. She was either writing with calligraphic precision onto a small placard, or mastering some ancient Swiss *gourmette* recipe. She usually had paint on her fingers or flour on her apron. It didn't matter if it was 11pm or 2am - this house was like New York, the city that never sleeps.

In June of 2008, I was at *CrossLiNK*, the au pair Bible study I helped lead alongside my *Youth for Christ* co-workers, and my emotions were charged. I was moving away from Switzerland in a few short weeks to serve as a missionary in South Africa, and grief was my constant companion. My car became my sanctuary during my ten-minute drive home on the dark, narrow streets. I sang my heart out, cried my eyes red, and pleaded with God for one small tangible thing that night: *"Jesus, I need a hug."*

I walked in the door to *The Goat Farm* in the wee hours of the night. I expected to sneak my way down the stairs to my basement bedroom, but as soon as I opened the door and stepped foot onto the red carpeted entryway, I saw Sharon standing right in front of me. It's as if she was anticipating my return at that exact moment. She caught the grief painted across my face and met my eyes with a question, "Do you need a hug?"

I fell into her tired and weepy, but feeling sure of God's tangible love. Sharon and I embraced and cried until we ran out of tears. God sent her to meet me with a hug in the wee hours of the night because

He knew that's exactly what I needed. He also knew I needed it from her.

Living with the Bentzens was like simultaneously being swept up in a giant cloud of warm, fuzzy love, juxtaposed with color, chaos, and the always-inviting and scintillating smells of delicious food. There was always something going on. Someone was always packing a bag for a trip to Africa or the United States, and someone was always awake, regardless of the hour.

I had a boyfriend back in my Swiss days, too. His name was Ollie and he was petite in stature with brown, black, and white fur. He was the family dog, and from the moment I stepped foot into *The Goat Farm*, he adopted me as his own. He followed me everywhere I went and greeted me every morning by walking the perimeter of my bed while rubbing his long, skinny nose across the dangling sheets. Ollie and I took walks in the forest every day. He was my sounding board on many occasions, and though he never barked advice back at me, his presence was always enough.

Presence.

It's been eight years since I lived with the Bentzens, but their presence still lingers with me. When I think of them, my heart moves. They gave me so much during my time in Switzerland - food on the table, a car to drive, a home to live in, and a deep sense of family and belonging. I feel the exact same way about my family and deep friendships that I've had across oceans and continents. I can go days, weeks, even years without seeing certain people, but true relationships have this one quality: *an ability to linger.*

When we are real, available and present with people, that's what happens. They linger with us. It's like walking into your favorite Mexican restaurant - you can smell your dining experience on your jacket days later. It lingers. It's tangible. It's identifiable. It's a reminder of good food, good people, and good times.

Back in 2013, I was on staff at a church in Texas that was intending to plant a church in London. Through a series of many events and connections, I was asked to be the Associate Pastor of the new church plant. I was to be trained for a six-week period in Texas and then sent off to assist in planting the church in London. After two weeks into my training, though, I debated walking away from the opportunity in front of me. There were complexities at play with the culture and priorities of the church and I was restless with anxiety. Everything in me wanted to run screaming from the confusion and deception I was encountering on a daily basis. In the dark quiet moments of one spring night, I listened to a sermon by one of my favorite pastors called *Linger Longer*.

The point that I took to heart and that kept me steadfast for the duration of my training was that sometimes when we linger, it allows God to do more in and through us. We want to run away when things get really hard, but He is working His purposes out by our willingness to linger. He is working behind the scenes and bringing things to light in the waiting.

That was a really challenging season of ministry life – one that left me shattered and broken when it finally ended in an unexpected, ugly way after a period of three months.

I didn't move back to London to plant a church, but God knew exactly what He was doing. My lingering there – when everything in me was running for the hills – brought some very important things to light. That same lingering shook leaves on branches that needed shaking in my own life and the lives of others involved in the church plant.

Lingering has purpose.

It reminds me of a budding relationship between two people. The date comes to an end, and yet the pregnant pause before the "goodnight" salutation communicates, "I want to know more. I want to spend more time with you. Does this have to end?" There's something spiritually profound that happens in lingering - it's like our souls are yearning for more.

That's what lingering does. It creates longing.

I think of all the places I've lived – France, Switzerland, South Africa, Australia, England, the United States – and I cannot help but feel overcome by God's goodness. Planting myself in cities around the world has allowed me to linger - to be present - in peoples' lives. It has allowed me to be real, to go deep, and truly connect with people from all over the world.

I have this odd habit when my time in a place is drawing to a close. I like to be *fully present* where I am. I neglect Skype calls from friends and family back home because I want to soak up every moment of every second of every day exactly where I am. This is a great practice, but it would be even better if I lived out that desire every single day. I want to wake up every morning and be fully present with every person that I encounter. I want to be someone who lingers with others.

But it hasn't just been about my lingering - it's been about others giving me the gift of their presence, too.

I know that my life is richer because of the presence of other people. Proximity isn't always the key. Presence is. When you see and love people for who they are, right where they are, that's presence. When you commit to walking through the hard days with people, that's presence. I can sit across the table from you and never be present, and you can sit beside me all day long and never gift me with your presence.

Presence is full of intention and purpose. It lingers.

And yes, time changes the depth and weight of that lingering, but inevitably people who linger become part of you while you become part of them. I think of all the lingering people over the course of my lifetime. I am blown away by God's goodness and graciousness in connecting me with family and friends globally that continue to linger in my heart because where there is lingering, there is longing. And there, presence is found… and maybe a late night hug, too.

CHAPTER 19

The Hands of God

"Surprise me Lord, as a seed surprises itself." ~ *George Herbert*

London has a hold on my soul. The diversity of culture, flavors, and sounds that echo through the city are mesmerizing and magnetic. Around every corner is a new face with a new story to tell. In every story, there is a declaration of God. Is He near? Is He far? Is He working and moving?

In October of 2011, I was at a conference in London and had gone from my dinner table to make myself a cup of tea. As I was waiting to rifle through my various tea options, I bantered with the woman next to me.

"Oh, you definitely shouldn't pick that tea. It's moldy and green."

She started laughing and then replied, "Yes, I think I'll just go for boring stuff. English Breakfast."

This casual back-and-forth opened the way for a friendly conversation. After learning that this lovely woman was at this conference center for a women's retreat, I jokingly commented, "Oh, so you'll be doing facials, massages, and painting each others' fingernails?"

To my surprise she answered, "Actually, yes. In fact, they've brought me in to facilitate all the spa treatments."

Oh, what a joyous and convenient connection I had just made!

I continued with my jovial tone and said, "Well, if you need a guinea pig to practice on, I'll happily make myself available!"

She smirked and then paused for a few seconds, as if searching for something. I stood next to her in silence. Then with conviction she smiled said, "God has told me that I need to give you a massage. He is so very good to us. Yes, that's right. This is a divine appointment; I will give you a massage."

I was taken aback at such a strange offer, but also wildly excited by this turn in the conversation and even more thrilled about the prospect of a free massage. We chatted for a moment more, and then agreed upon the time and place for this wonderful gift.

I was unfamiliar with this side of God's nature. I entered into conversation with my new friend and roommate at the conference, and was joking with her about my free massage. I never would have dreamed that God would be involved in something like this, or that He would even care about such a small detail in the story of my own life.

This particular trip to London in 2011 came on the back of a dark season in my life. I had just jumped from the "top of the world" at Hillsong College in Australia into the "valley of the forgotten" in my hometown in Texas. Part of the reason for that is because I had just spent two years in Australia where God performed radical heart surgery on me in preparation to be used by Him as a woman in ministry. During the course of my years abroad in France, Switzerland, South Africa, and Australia, I had been exposed to different expressions of Christian faith, which included watching women excel creatively as leaders in a variety of ministries. They weren't just leading children's and women's ministries; they were creative pioneers and fire starters for movements to stand on the front line as the hands and feet of Jesus in fighting human trafficking, empowering women of all shapes and sizes, and serving the vulnerable in tangible ways. Being back in Texas felt daunting because my lens of the world - and the way women fit into it – had been broadened. Jesus' words from Mark 6:6 rang true every time I was home:

"Jesus said to them, 'A prophet is not without honor except in his own town…'"

Growing up in the Bible-belt of North Texas ingrained a system of beliefs within me that I never questioned until I moved overseas for the first time. The unwritten rules of my culture were that it was encouraged to believe that anything was possible and accessible. But there was also an underlying message that told my heart – "anything is possible *unless you are a woman who feels called to ministry.*"

In the summer of my eighth grade year, I attended youth camp with 350 other pubescent teenagers. During a sweaty session beneath a non-air-conditioned tabernacle, I felt the tug of God on my heart. The voice from the stage was loud and clear, "God could call *you* to Africa!" Sitting on my folding chair trying to deny the strange warm fluttering in my heart, I repeated my desperate prayer as a chant: "God, please don't call *me* to Africa. Please don't call *me* to Africa. Please don't call *me* to Africa."

God has a hilarious sense of humor, doesn't He? Though my specific call to Africa only came years later, my twiggy legs carried me down the aisle that day to the front of the stage to meet face-to-face with the camp speaker. I had already become a Christ-follower in my earlier years, but this rush to the front of the tabernacle was the next step for me: answering a call to missions, and the even bigger seeming impossibility, answering the call to be a *woman in ministry.*

At thirteen years old, I really didn't understand what that meant. In fact, I had a very limited idea of what that *could* look like. I visualized my pastor's perfectly-coiffed sweet wife sitting quietly next to her husband, golf-clapping and smiling in support of him. This was not a bad thing because she was an incredibly godly woman, but it just wasn't how I saw myself as a "woman in ministry." In fact, I pictured myself in her place, feeling constrained as if I had a piece of tape stuck over my mouth. That horrified me! I also visualized a woman with wild hair chasing wildebeests out of her vegetable garden in the savannahs of Africa. She was dressed in a long robe, her face pale without makeup, and her voice strange with the utterances of a tribal tongue. I pictured myself in her place, with a baby on each hip feeling suffocated in the deserts of Africa. I didn't see myself as either.

Maybe that's all dramatic, but growing up in a Baptist church in the 1980s helped shape my understanding of being a woman in ministry. Admittedly, it was limited. Now, because my life has unfolded in an entirely different way, I understand that God is much bigger than my limited understanding of Him and the way He uses women to build His kingdom on earth as it is in heaven. This is a huge part of my own story and personal journey.

God cares about the details of our lives. He cares when we don't think He sees us or understands us. He cares enough to show us Himself in creative and unexpected ways. He cares enough to take us along the journey with Him. He cares enough to use our gifts and passions for His purposes in this world... regardless of whether we are male or female.

In fact, my pastor said something recently that struck a chord deep in my heart. He said, "Where God is advanced, the value and position of women is advanced." How true! Jesus made women visible in a day and age where they were otherwise unseen and undervalued by the confines of culture.

I was doing a study on the genealogy of Jesus from the book of Matthew. In a time when only men were listed, five women are mentioned as part of the bloodline of Jesus – Tamar, Rahab, Ruth, Bathsheba, and Mary. All of these women had their own stories. One prostituted herself to her father-in-law and another was a prostitute. One was a foreign widow, another a king's wife, and finally, a young virgin. The thread that ties these women together is the love and redemption of a God who sees women and places value on them. Despite their imperfections, they are part of the lineage of the Son of God, Jesus. How marvelous is that, and how marvelous it is that God deemed it important enough to include in His Holy Word?

God uses women in special ways.

When I knocked on the door of my new friend's beauty room late that evening for my free massage, I anticipated that God would show up in a major way. After all, He's the one who orchestrated this divine appointment.

I walked into the room, which smelled of lovely oils and incense, and Maureen, my new friend and masseuse, asked me to lie on the bed in preparation for my massage. She gently walked over to me as I was lying on my stomach and boldly invited the Holy Spirit to be a part of our time together.

The moments that ensued felt ethereal. I relaxed into what felt like nothingness, while Maureen used her hands as the literal hands of God. She kept whispering over me, "new anointing, fresh fire," and as her hands grazed over my rock-like shoulders and stiff neck, she declared that I carried a heavy mantle for the sake of Christ and His glory. She said that God was sanding and refining the precious, solid wood of this mantle and that it was similar to an antique tower that had been a place of refuge for many.

Words can't do an experience like this justice. As I lay prostrate in the beauty room that day, I knew that God was with us, that His Presence was undeniable, and Maureen's worn fingers were the tangible reminder of His love and grace over my life that day.

After the massage, Maureen sat near me and flicked through the pages of her well-loved Bible and read the following from Isaiah 58:11-12 over me:

"The Lord will guide you always; He will satisfy your needs in a sun-scorched land and will strengthen your frame. You will be like a well-watered garden, like a spring whose waters never fail. Your people will rebuild the ancient ruins and will raise-up the age old foundations; you will be called repairer of broken walls, restorer of streets with dwellings."

She then read the whole of Psalm 139.

I felt peace, molding, refining, and the power of the Holy Spirit in those moments literally forcing out the knots and kinks of my life. As she continued to declare hope against anxiety and doubt, my faith rose up within me and I began to remember the faithfulness of God and the many wonders He had done in my life. Because He is God, He will do it again! I felt him gently guiding me out of the "valley of the forgotten" back into a safe place of knowing Him, and being known by Him. He reminded me of my calling as a woman in ministry that day, and I felt Him relighting a fire within my bones to be brave and bold in using my God-given gifts. I was ready to build, pioneer, and do whatever it took to be all that God had called me to be.

Reflecting on that bizarre, yet undeniable gift of a massage from God, I realize that sometimes it literally takes the hands of another to stir and revive our faith. It was such an encouragement to me, beyond what I gained personally, to know that this brave woman of God would bring what she had to be used by God.

I had never met a prophetic masseuse. The story of Maureen's life spoke of a God who was near, a God who wants to use all of who we are. I learned that it doesn't matter what your gift or passion is – it's simple to use it for God. It may require boldness and bravery, but God provides that. He wants us to use what we have for His glory.

So whether you are a writer, singer, teacher, cook, bus driver, masseuse, poet, business owner, actor, accountant, stay-at-home parent or a *woman* - use your gift for God. It's as simple as tuning into His voice and letting Him schedule your appointments. Let Him surprise you with unexpected moments of His goodness, in ways that you never thought or saw possible. Let Him use every gift you have for His purposes.

"May we be Your hands, O God."

CHAPTER 20

The Kiss of Alan

"It is never too late to be what you might have been." ~ George Eliot

"What I do will never determine who I am, but who I am will determine what I do." ~ Bethany's journal, July 2012

In November of 2012, I had an unforgettable day. It was a seemingly normal Sunday. Working for an amazing church on the outskirts of London, I was accustomed to teaching Bible studies and leading worship during the evening services, but this was a day in which I saw God begin to visually outwork His Promise over my life in the particular area of my calling to preach. Yes, that's right. I'm a woman and I'm talking about the "p" word: PREACHING.

You see, with each country and continent, with each season and step, God has revealed His plans for my future in small swallow-able doses. I've had glimpses here and there, as well as opportunities that have affirmed the seeds and passions rooted deep within the soil of my heart. In Bible College, I realized that I had this fire burning within my bones to preach. That sounds dramatic, I know, but the discovery of my passion dropped like a penny when one of my pastors unpacked Jeremiah 20:9: *"But if I say, 'I will not mention him or speak any more in his name,' his word is in my heart like a fire, a fire shut up in my bones. I am weary of holding it in; indeed, I cannot."*

The next fourteen months were spent swimming through the rough seas of doubt, wondering if I could actually preach. Every excuse invaded my mind. *You're a woman. You don't have a seminary degree. What do you have to say anyway? You're too young. But you grew up Southern Baptist.* The list went on and on.

God is funny like that. He lets us wallow in our self-doubt at times, so that He can raise us up at just the right time. As with most circumstances in my life, I took it as an opportunity to learn to trust Him fully.

This particular Sunday He had sent me to a small English church. I was *the* preacher for the service that morning, and it was my first time preaching outside of my Bible college environment.

Fear gripped me the night before. In fact, panic woke me hour upon hour with that salty taste in my mouth, the warning sign that your body sends when you need to vomit. I thrashed in my bed all night, fighting the voices in my head. *You're a woman, you can't preach. No one cares what you have to say. You don't have a clue what you're doing. You're going to choke.*

My eyes were heavy upon waking from my doubt-encumbered sleep, but my spirit was strong and ready to face the day. Or so I thought.

I arrived at the church early and sat in my warm car for fifteen minutes, too paralyzed to get out, knowing that I was responsible for hearing from God and communicating it in a way that others could understand. This totally freaked me out. It's not like I was talking on behalf of my mom, or my friend, or even my boss. My faint little voice was there to speak something of God, *the* Almighty God.

Thankfully another car eventually pulled up next to me and shocked me out of my over-analysis mode, jarring me to exit my car quickly. Surely it would be off-putting for them to see the preacher girl looking like a white ghost sitting in her car talking to herself. I wanted to give a better first impression than that. I didn't want to scare them away before I had even uttered a word.

Shaky legs ushered me into a small room, where I was immediately offered a cup of tea and a seat on the front row by my kind hostess. Moments later the service started and my nerves slowly dissipated.

Then the drum roll pounded (in my head), and I was *on*.

I stood at the podium, my notes displayed in front of me. I opened my mouth and traveled to some place I can't really recall.

When you're doing the thing you are created to do, time glides by like a warm knife cutting through butter. It felt like time passed so smoothly and quickly, and before I knew it, my notebook was closed and I was seated back on the front row.

I had just spoken with full passion about how God breathes life into our dry places, even when we turn our backs on Him. And I'm glad I have my notes because I hardly remember any word I spoke.

What I do remember is that at the close of the service, several church members approached me to share their gratitude for my words. As I was packing up my things after these encouraging conversations, I noticed a short elderly man who was hunched over and wearily standing in front of me. With caution, he extended his hand at the speed of molasses, placing it in mine, and tilted his head upwards to catch my gaze. I bent down to meet his. He struggled to form the words, *"My name is Alan. My eyes were closed the whole time you were preaching, not because I was sleeping, but because I wanted to soak in every word you said. Every single word mattered. Thank you for being God's voice today."* Then with his toothless grin, he lowered his head again, eloquently kissed my hand and waddled away.

In that moment, tears raged inside me, so I quickly thanked the church leadership, said goodbye to the church members, and dashed out the door to make the thirty-minute drive back to my English cottage.

Along the route, cheeks soaked with tears of gratitude for the events of the morning, I heard God's whisper cut through the noise of my mind: "I AM ALAN AND I AM KISSING YOUR HAND."

This memory is tucked away in the deepest part of my heart, because when I teach, preach, write, sing, or create, I do it for Alan. I do it for God and I do it for you, too.

What a joy and privilege, what a humbling blessing it is to be the mouthpiece of God and to declare words of life, so that He can breathe His life back into the dry and dusty places of our lives.

This, too, is for Alan.

Chapter 21

Don't Watch Your Step

"Therefore, if anyone is in Christ, he is a new creation. The old has passed away... the new has come!" ~ 2 Corinthians 5:17 (ESV)

I had the opportunity to paint flesh once. That probably sounds somewhat disturbing. It is. It was, and it interrupted my entire pattern of thinking.

I was on a mission trip to Den Haag in the Netherlands serving with four English women in a very low-key church environment. We spent our days meeting with neighbors and churchgoers, listening to stories of doubt, confusion, pain, and loss. We were in the heart of a low-income neighborhood and the people we met had real tangible needs. Many of them had sordid pasts and were trying to take steps towards a better future.

In the course of a week, we had an array of first-time experiences. We stood in the streets one night as the pastor of the church we were working with went outside to break up a violent dogfight among neighbors, one of which was a church member. We spent one afternoon in the home of a couple that had two children with severe disabilities and lived on a tight income, which barely covered their medical expenses. They weren't proclaimed Christ-followers yet, but they found a solace and refuge from their hard lives at this little church in Den Haag that met in the living room of the pastor's home.

Real life pushed in on every moment for this community.

This pastor couple had a very simple home with one bathroom that they shared with an entire congregation of people. They also had a large pet rabbit that hopped around, using the entire house as his litter box. We had to watch our every step!

Life here was like that metaphorically speaking. This was life's litter box. Bad, smelly life stuff was lying discarded all over the floor. The people who came here were hurt, broken, and crying for help. Most people had been watching "their every step" around them for their entire lives.

But, not here. Not at this church. This was a place where they *belonged*.

I had never seen the Christian ethos of "belong-behave-believe" outworked so authentically with such a depth of love and grace. The emphasis was that people, all people – dirty, smelly, sex-addicts, drug-addicts, drunks, abusers, thieves, broken, messy, hurting people – belonged here. They weren't expected to *behave* or *believe* first; they *belonged*. This place had an open door policy that shouted: *our home is your home because this is where Jesus lives*. This Body of Christ was enmeshed in the community, whispering hope in crisis moments, all centered around a lifestyle of *gospel love*, not gospel convenience. There was nothing glamorous about a church setting like this; it was ugly, hard, and nitty-gritty. The beauty of God's redemption in these raw, vulnerable lives struck me.

That aspect was made real to me when I painted flesh one day during our trip.

We spent two days painting the walls of the home of a former prostitute, Lucy. She had just turned her back on this form of income and was still very jaded from many years of emotional abuse and neglect. She struggled to receive love, even in small doses, and though she asked the pastor if we could paint her home, she fought our help with every ounce she could muster.

Despite this, we persisted in love and grace.

She busied herself for the day and gave us space to be in her home alone to paint. We prayed and sang worship music over her home and life as we painted the walls the color of peach flesh.

Mesmerized by this pale, orangey color, I was quick to judge it by thinking that I would never choose it for my home. And just as I had that thought, God's words were plain in my heart, "Lucy didn't choose this color; I did. I am painting her walls with the same color I am painting her life: new flesh."

I was sobered by this thought. God had invited me to be a part of this woman's story of renewal and a fresh beginning. Just as her walls were flesh, He was covering her old flesh with new, clean, healthy flesh. He is the God of redemption. He is a God that replaces the old with the new. He is a God that covers your sin, my sin, and the sins of everyone we know with His love, compassion, and mercy.

And when He looks upon us, He doesn't see the past. He doesn't see our hang-ups and our mistakes. He doesn't see imperfection. He sees new flesh. He sees new life because He has painted us with His flesh, His life.

I was so honored to be a part of a group of women that gave up their time and energy to serve this community in the Netherlands. I was even more grateful for the pastor couple that gave their lives to make sure people know Jesus loves them and calls them to come just as they are. Jesus welcomes the dirty, smelly, sex-addicts, drug-addicts, drunks, abusers, thieves, broken, messy, and the hurting. He welcomes all people. Jesus doesn't "watch His step" around them. He is their home, and in Him, they always belong first.

DOWN UNDER: South Africa & Australia

CHAPTER 22

Voices

"The evening sings in a voice of amber, the dawn is surely coming." ~ Al Stewart

In the summer of 2007, I told my pastor that I knew God was going to change my life in Africa. "It's going to be more than just the confrontation of poverty and AIDS. *I know God is literally going to change my life.*" This was a strange comment to make, considering that I lived and worked in Switzerland at the time.

Shortly after that conversation, though, in the mysterious way that God does, He opened the door for me to travel to South Africa. In October, three months after my declaration to my pastor, I was on a plane from Geneva to Johannesburg to meet members of my Texas church worship team, including my dad. Before the plane even pulled up to the gate, Africa infected me. The music over the plane speakers was a meshing of drumbeats and tribal chants, and my heart danced to their rhythms. It was love at first sound.

I exited the airport into a land filled with life, color, and culture. I walked to the waiting van in a dreamlike state. I was ready for this mission trip because my heart was full of expectancy for what God was going to do in and through us in this beautiful country.

He didn't disappoint.

We spent our days playing with AIDS orphans, teaching in schools, talking with people in townships, and leading worship at local churches. After our first worship service at a church in East London, our van driver, Leo, approached my dad. He said, "My wife, Linda, whispered something to me while your daughter, Bethany, was leading worship. She said, 'If God gave me a voice like that, I'd go anywhere in the world for Him.'"

My dad repeated Linda's comment to me later that night. When he told me what she had said, I lit up from the inside out. Her words were like electricity to my soul.

I didn't really know what I was searching for at the time. I guess I was a little bit like a kid fumbling in the dark for a light-switch she knows is there, but can't find. I had been living with an unsettled pit in my stomach for months. The peace was slowly leaking from my life. I didn't know the source of the leak, and I was unsure of how to stop it.

What I knew is that Linda's words reverberated in my heart. They gave me clarity. I had newfound purpose and meaning. Her simple one-sentence comment summarized the desire of my whole existence.

I love this about God. Linda, a stranger to me then (although she'd come to be one of my "soul friends" in just one short year), was the voice of God in my life. She started that pattern before we even met, and continues to speak His truth over my life, even across the oceans that now separate us. In fact, we were talking recently about moving her family overseas to give them a chance at a better future. We had a conversation about bravery and the fact that risking everything for God is always worth it. Mid-conversation, she spoke something over me that I needed to hear in that exact moment. She said, "I know without a shadow of a doubt that BRAVE and BETHANY are one and the same."

God's timing is always perfect, and His voice so strongly resonates through His people.

A couple of days after Linda's comment to Leo arrested my heart, I sat in the pew of a small church in Cape Town after having just led worship. My mission pastor, Bryan, preached about the life of Gideon and about two tests that suddenly appear when God speaks His vision into your life: 1. Fear, and 2. Distraction. He went on to say that he had often pondered about Gideon's response to God calling him out to be a mighty warrior. He pointed out that Gideon didn't verbally doubt God with the common human insecurity of, "Why me?" Bryan then said something that radically shifted my perspective: "I believe Gideon didn't ask, 'Why me?' because *deep down, he wanted to be a mighty warrior.*"

This short statement brought everything into a perfectly timed collision of revelation. My thoughts were like rapid-fire: *Could it be that God wants me to use my voice? Could it be that it's not just something I want to do, but something that He created me to do?*

In thinking about Gideon's call to be a mighty warrior, I knew in that moment that my "mighty warrior" calling was to: *Go anywhere in the world to use my voice for Him.*

The words of a stranger had brought clarity to my life, and the words from a friend had wrapped it neatly in a bow. God's words penetrated my heart through these fellow believers.

My trip only escalated from this point. God just kept showing off His goodness, grace, and purpose for my time in South Africa. He kept gently whispering that He was *changing my life.*

In fact, at one point, our team was driving over a small mountain on the outskirts of Cape Town. As we came around the corner into the town of Glen Cairn, I had my ear-buds in and was leaning against the van window listening to worship music when my spirit was jolted with one word that rattled repeatedly in my heart and mind: *home.* I had an undeniable sense of peace and comfort that this was "home" in that moment, and yet I immediately jumped into doubt. *This is ridiculous. I live in Switzerland. Why would this feel like home?*

Fast forward exactly one year, and I was living at the base of that same mountain in Glen Cairn, South Africa, where I first heard the word, *home.*

Suffice it to say that this trip had been completely life changing. Though the trip was "officially" over, I stayed on a few extra days with my dad while he had business meetings in Cape Town.

I sat down to ponder my life. Everything was shifting. My Swiss visa had expired two months before my trip to South Africa, and was currently in an appeal process for renewal. This wasn't an easy process, and approval wasn't a shoe-in. I was baffled.

I loved my life in Switzerland. I had rich friendships, and a thriving ministry that was reaching au pairs from all over the world. I loved snowboarding and leading worship at my international church. I loved my Swiss family and the fresh baguettes and cheese on Sunday mornings from the French market.

There was so much at stake, but I couldn't deny it. I knew God was on the move, and I sensed He was about to change my address yet again.

That sense stemmed from the crazy ways in which God was working in my life in South Africa, but it was also a reflection of what was beginning to happen around me in Switzerland.

I am deeply, unapologetically relational. It is a great blessing, and, at times, my greatest struggle. I hate goodbyes, and yet, that's been my so-called "thorn in the flesh" of my travels and years.

In fact, when fear creeps into my heart, it's usually around the thought of having to say goodbye to people I love and cherish. That fear is justified because it has been the story of my life. I've lived in six countries on four continents, which has required countless hellos and goodbyes, and yet, God's love and mercy has encompassed me every time I have surrendered by speaking that dreaded "goodbye" to someone I love dearly.

Because I am wired this way, and because I've moved around so much, I have an accurate honing device that clues me into the "shift of a season." When I know God is about to rock my world by uprooting me yet again, He begins "conditioning" me away from a place. The puzzle pieces of my life don't fit so easily anymore. I lose motivation for the work in front of me. Conversations oftentimes feel labored.

One of the biggest warning signs of "coming change" is when the voices in my life, those of my inner-circle, co-workers, and church friends, stop carrying so much weight. People who've represented the voice of God in my life no longer align with where I feel God is leading my heart. But when this happens, He always starts raising others up who speak words that resonate with what I sense I'm hearing from Him.

When a wave of new voices of mentors, pastors, and friends arises, my ears perk-up because I know God is on the move. This doesn't mean that the voices in the current place and season are null and void; it just means that my heart is shifting and new voices are empowering me for the next thing in the next place. This is exactly what was happening through Linda and Bryan in South Africa. I thought two strong voices were enough for this trip. I was wrong.

God had others lined-up.

My dad and I were invited by a local pastor to a tiny church that stood atop Red Hill, just above Glen Cairn and Simonstown near Cape Town. The small building was constructed of tin and old wooden slabs, and sat tilted on the red ground. We made our way inside, which was the size of a small bedroom, and sat in white plastic chairs two rows from the front. The pastor immediately walked up to us, introduced himself, and welcomed us to the service. Then, without pause, he asked, "What will you be sharing with us today?" We had been in several churches during our time in South Africa, so we were used to the expectation that we would be sharing something with the congregation. So, I sheepishly told him that I could sing, and the smile on his face widened.

"Great, you can sing for us when I call you to the front."

As soon as he walked away to start the service, though, all the confidence in me faded away. I felt completely unworthy to be there in that dilapidated building. My story wasn't one of struggle, but one of abundance. My story wasn't one of pain and neglect, but one of community and God's goodness. *Who was I to share anything with these people?*

My doubts were confirmed as I sat and listened to church member after church member share stories of God's miraculous healing powers. One lady talked about how the doctor told her three weeks ago that she was HIV positive, and when she went back to see him over the weekend, he said she was healed. Another woman talked about praying with a Muslim woman who had a very serious leg wound. She was healed on the spot while they rode the train together.

I didn't know where I was or how I got there, but I knew that God was in this place. This falling-down building housed the immense glory of God Almighty. His presence was rich and tangible. I felt completely overwhelmed and unworthy to even be sitting in a chair next to these incredible people of God.

Fortunately, my doubts and feeling of unworthiness didn't control my actions that day. The pastor wouldn't let them. He announced loudly to the congregation, "We have a very special gift for you today. Our sister from America is going to sing for us. Come on up,

Bethany."

I smiled politely, though I was a total mess on the inside, and asked God to give me His strength. I stood and walked towards the front. When I opened my mouth to sing one of my favorite worship songs, *There is a Day*, all of my emotions and the nearness of God collided in the tones leaping from my voice. The sound that came out was different; it was stronger, more transparent, and more authentic.

After I sang, the pastor told the congregation: "The amazing thing about God's kingdom is that blessings from Him are free, and He uses His people to bless the kingdom. You would've had to pay 100 Rand to hear what we've heard today for free."

I sat coyly on the front row until the end of the service, when a man came to me and took my hands in his and spoke over me, "God told me today that He is raising you up to lead His people in worship, tens of thousands of people in your generation and beyond. I see in you creativity and passion, and you must not fear. You must not hold back. You must break-through, for God is mighty and He is powerful. There will be challenges, but you must open your ears and tune into Him. He will always lead you."

He was already leading me, and He was already "conditioning" me towards change. When I arrived back to Switzerland, things in my work and ministry felt more challenging, but God was also confirming my calling to use my voice for Him. I got several invitations to lead worship and speak in different places, and I trusted that God knew exactly what He was doing in my life.

Just two months after my trip to South Africa, I got word that my visa for another year in Switzerland had been denied. Two weeks later I got a phone call from my pastor, Bryan. He said, "Bethany, are you sitting down?" This kind of question always jarred me, especially from him, so I *did* sit down. He then said, "How do you feel about moving to South Africa to lead worship?"

I knew from the moment the words came out of his mouth that my answer needed to be "yes." It was as clear as crystal. God was at work. He was moving, shifting, stirring, and my address was definitely going to be changing.

Despite all of the obvious factors at play during this time of my life, it took me another full month to say a whole-hearted "yes" to this new opportunity in front of me. It wasn't the "yes" that was difficult; it was the "no" to my Swiss life that was the hard part.

When we say "yes" to one thing, it always requires "no" to another. I wasn't ready to let go of the life I had loved, even though I knew God was working.

Fortunately, He was patient with me.

In the time in-between the news of my Swiss visa denial and the offer in South Africa, I traveled back to Texas for a family wedding. As I spoke with friends and family about my looming decision, they all spoke to me as if I had already decided to move to South Africa.

This is another way that God "conditions" me for change. People around me begin to speak, almost prophetically, about my life and future. It's as if they see something that I can't yet – or *won't* yet – see.

The thing is, I *knew* eventually that I'd say yes. I wasn't scared to say "yes" to South Africa, but I didn't yet have the courage to say "no" to Switzerland. And until I was ready to do both, I sat paralyzed by indecision.

When I returned back to Switzerland in early January of 2008, I had a meeting with my boss, who had just recently resigned from his position. Our relationship had been somewhat rocky with all the unknowns that were pervading both of our lives, but our lunch meeting that day was God-ordained. My conversation with my boss catapulted me into the bravery and courage that I was lacking.

He spoke freely with me: "It's time to move on, Bethany, and you have to be okay with that. It's time to say "yes," to put words to the sense of calling you have about South Africa." I walked away with an understanding that I wasn't responsible for what I was leaving behind, but I *was* responsible for the obedience ahead.

I went home, picked-up the phone and put my "yes" on the table.

I've always been captivated by the fact that God spoke creation into existence. He speaks and life appears. He speaks and stars shine. He speaks and oceans roar. He speaks and mountains peak. He speaks and hearts are transformed.

I love that He graciously gifts imperfect and wayward humans with the ability to speak on His behalf as well. I hear God in many ways — through nature, beauty, circumstances, Scripture, in dreams, and in personal prayer — but I know that His voice is often the loudest through others. For that, I am thankful.

Chapter 23

Expectancy is Abstract Art

"Always be in a state of expectancy, and see that you leave room for God to come in as He likes." ~ Oswald Chambers

I escaped the blistering heat of Texas in 2008 to move to the chilly temperatures of a South African winter. My purpose in leaping overseas, yet again, was to lead worship at a church in East London, which sits on the stunning coast of South Africa's pristine and unadulterated beaches.

I moved there with six boxes of my belongings in-tow, which signified my commitment to serve there for at least the full time my visa allowed, three years.

A young, bubbly couple, Leo and Linda O'Connor, met me at the airport with their toddler, Thomas. After loading my giant American-sized bags into the car, they whisked me away to the home of Leo's parents, my own personal Bed and Breakfast, for my induction into the events of weekly *braai night*. Sleepy eyes hung on my face, but the smells of the grill and the flavors of South African food kept me awake. After such warm hospitality, I was stuffed to the brim with food and new friendship, and so I headed to my hot pink and white bedroom, which was accented with orchids and the smell of sunshine. I slept like a baby.

The next morning I awoke to a breakfast fit for a queen, made with love by Eunice, the family housekeeper. She was shy and gentle, and giggled profusely when I thanked her repeatedly for the glorious spread of toast, jam, eggs and cereal on the table before me.

That day felt normal for me, and so quickly. Because it was a holiday in South Africa, Leo and Linda picked me up and took me to a family festival in the same park where they had their wedding photos taken just a few years before. It was cool outside, but the view of the sea was breathtakingly beautiful. I can still remember the smell of the air and the sound of children's laughter cutting across the breeze.

In that beautiful park on that crisp September day, though, I learned something that shook me from my perfect little entrance into South Africa. My new pastor and boss, the catalyst in bringing me all the way from Texas, was on an extended leave for personal reasons. This was the first I was hearing of any of this. I had just moved thousands of miles, across oceans and deserts, and now my go-to person wasn't even around to guide me in starting my new job in this foreign place. Suddenly, I had no idea why I had moved my whole life to South Africa.

As if it wasn't difficult enough that my point person was not around, to my surprise as the week unfolded, I found out the elders at the church weren't even aware of the plans for me to serve at the church. I had moved my life from Switzerland, leaving friends and community behind, with the intent of serving in Africa for at least three years. All of a sudden, my bubble was popped and I felt totally blindsided by what was happening to me. Less than twenty-four hours of being on the ground, my perfect little African adventure was rapidly unraveling.

In the days and weeks that followed, I was acutely aware that I had come to Africa with *expectations*, the linear outworking of my plans and dreams. I had taken the gift of this opportunity to serve and tied it up nicely and neatly in my mind with a pretty little pink ribbon. I grabbed this thing that God initiated and convinced myself that it would work out exactly this way and that, neglecting to consider what He wanted for this time and season in South Africa. I never stopped to consider that He might have different plans for my time there.

In my head, things were supposed to go a certain way. They were supposed to unfold according to my script. I arrived with spirit and pizzazz for this new adventure, and God graciously taught me that I needed to reposition myself before Him with something deceivingly similar to expectation, but something completely different: *expectancy*.

Expectancy declares, "God, I need You. I want You to move. I am letting go of the way I think things should go and surrendering because I know You will orchestrate what is best over what is just good." Expectation is dangerously linear and lined-out with bullet points and sub-categories, with little boxes to tick off that bolster a feeling of productivity.

Expectancy is abstract art. Expectation is paint-by-numbers.

I realized that if I were going to thrive in this season, I was going to have to learn that God had the reins and was plotting His course for me. It would be in my best interest to surrender to His will for my life, instead of coercing things to happen my way in my timing. Unfortunately, I'm all too good at that and, therefore, this thing called "surrender" never comes easily for me.

Sure, I've lived in lots of places away from friends and family and have, therefore, had to surrender relationships, community, stability, finances, and those things that might be considered as part of the "American Dream" (i.e. white picket fence, nice house, husband, 2.5 children, and the perfect family dog). Funnily enough, it's never felt like surrender because God has always blessed me tenfold in my endeavors. He has provided free housing, cars, and food. He has also blessed me with deep friendships in the various international soils where I have planted myself.

But this surrender in Africa felt different. It felt like a sideways sucker-punch. It shook me to my core and caused every doubt and uncertainty to spring up out of me with the force of a whale spouting water through its blowhole. It was different. It was hard. And the journey of my "wilderness" season had only just begun.

I was able to get past the gloom and the grime, the doubt and uncertainty of living and serving in a place where I no longer had any expectation for what I was going to do or who I was going to become. That was the ironic beauty in all of it. I was finally in a place of total surrender, and that meant God could sweep in and do what He wanted with me in Africa. My life was solely His. He was free to use me in any way He pleased.

In October of 2008, I wrote a journal entry that speaks to this surrender amidst uncertainty:

My God, my God... what are you teaching me in all of this? Why am I here? I come with a sense of expectancy — what will You do? Who will I become? I have that peace that passes all understanding, even amidst the chaos. Change takes time. Transition hurts. But it is necessary. Because I don't actually want a life of comfort. I want a Christ-centered, love-spewing life. Not an existence. But a creative life, full of God-inspiration and passion. I want to connect people to God. For God. Always God. I want to see God's glory shine out above all. Discomfort is the avenue I travel. Joy in Him is my destination.

Those months birthed in me endurance and tenacity I never had before. It was like being on a merry-go-round spinning full speed ahead while having the ability to keep from getting dizzy. This was a supernatural gift from God, not a skill I possessed apart from His grace and nearness in my every day life.

With every unexpected twist and turn that appeared in the days that followed, I was positioned to navigate the roads with resilience and strength. I look back to the days just before and after arriving in South Africa and see clearly that God had to wipe my human-tainted expectations away so that He could replace them with His Master plans. God's purposes always go beyond what we can see.

My time in South Africa was one of the most difficult ten-month seasons in my life up that point as a twenty-eight-year-old missionary. Yet, it was one of the most blessed. It was a season that marked me and defined me. I saw God deep in the eyes of the broken and hurting and in the tears of the dying and desolate. I felt His touch through the sticky, yet joyful embraces of children living in poverty. I heard His perfect unity in the powerful voices of former foes joining together to sing His praises in the townships. I smelled His beauty in the ocean breeze. I tasted His goodness in the unique flavors of that land. I saw God - in black, in white, in colors, in sadness, in joy, in fast, in slow, in nothingness, in abundance, in pain, in healing, in music, in silence, in brokenness, in redemption. I saw God. God is alive, and He was with me every single step of the way blowing my expectations out of the water with His unending grace, love, and goodness.

I heard it said once, *"change of pace + change of place = change of perspective."* I find this to be true anytime I travel overseas to make my home in a new place. I find it to be true when I'm waiting for God to move, when I naively try to predict His next step with my limited human perspective. I am always humbled by His unpredictability and the way His Sovereignty catches me off-guard in such wonderful, electrifying ways.

My time in South Africa was nothing short of unpredictable. I moved from city to city across the country doing ministry wherever needed, and I clearly saw the hand of God at work in placing me exactly where He wanted me when He wanted me to be there. He knew the individuals that needed an extra dose of love, connection, and a bit of craziness from a traveling Texas missionary. For the record, nothing that happened in South Africa fit my linear expectations. I may not have jotted those expectations onto paper, but they were engrained in my thinking, my heart, and my understanding of God through my filter of previous travel and life experiences. None of these things came to pass in the way I expected. But, God worked and moved in mysterious ways. He did His "thing" and moved my life like a pawn on a chessboard. He was the Grandmaster of the chessboard, and I, the surrendered pawn. His strategy was clear and concise, but I had no understanding of when, how, or where He would make His next move. I moved where He moved me. I stayed where He rested me. I adventured across the board of life as He led me. It was the most daunting, thrilling, scary, beautiful time of my life. The unknown taunted me, but I stood firm in that uncertainty because I knew He was in control. He was the Grandmaster and I had relinquished every part of my life to Him.

That season of life taught me to approach God with a mindset that asks, "*What adventure do YOU have in store today*," rather than laying out my plans for Him and asking Him to join me. I realized that He had already asked me to join Him a long time ago, and as believers, our *first* "yes" to Him is our biggest. All that God wants from us is our one big "yes" that declares that we trust Him and will follow Him wherever He leads us, whether that be to our neighbor's backyard, or to our child's teacher, to the polite stranger sitting next to us in our local coffee shop, or to an unreached people group on the other side of the world. He wants our "yes," which shouts, "I am filled with expectancy of all that you're going to do here, God! I may not understand it. It may not go as *I* planned, but I trust that you know exactly when, how, and where you want to use me. Here am I, Lord, send me."

Then I heard the voice of the Lord saying, "Whom shall I send? And who will go for us?" And I said, "Here am I. Send me!" ~ Isaiah 6:8

Concerning the mysterious ways of God, I have learned to cast aside all linear expectations, and instead posture myself before Him with a melodic anthem of expectancy.

Chapter 24

Leo-'ello

His master replied, "Well done, good and faithful servant!"
~ Matthew 25:21 (NIV)

To his face, I never called Leo by his name. To me, he was "Leo-'ello?" That's how he answered his phone, so that's what I assumed he wanted to be called.

Leo was more than a friend to me. He was my South African big brother, three years my senior. We even fought like siblings sometimes (I mean not that my brothers and I ever fought!). After I moved back to Texas from Africa, he and his wife, Linda, equally like a sister to me, visited over Christmas in 2009. His teasing had me at my breaking point one evening, so I retaliated by presenting his South African-self with a challenge to eat as many fresh jalapeños as he could at one meal. His pride, strong-will, and stubbornness accepted. Then I winked and put on a Southern drawl: "Great. I hope you feel the fire later."

He did. And pardon my French, but with a grimaced expression on his face, he mentioned that his rear-end resembled the flag of Japan.

That was Leo. There was something very magnetic about him. He also had this funny fascination with getting a reaction out of people. While I lived with them in South Africa, he would ask me to get my mom to send special *unmentionables* from Victoria's Secret for Linda when she sent my next care package. My mom always obliged, and Linda's reaction was always noteworthy, as marked by the hot pink on her cheeks.

One afternoon I was sitting in Leo's kitchen on a Skype call with my mission mentor back in Texas, discussing my finances and talking through prayer needs. We were in the middle of a serious chat, and Leo, to the soundtrack of Linda's laughter, came prancing into the kitchen wearing a yellow Speedo, and boasting a very awkward wedgie.

That was Leo. Bold. Confident. Hilarious.

But as wild and crazy as he was, he was also outrageously generous. Leo and Linda took me under their wings and gave me shelter in their home during my time as a missionary in East London, South Africa in 2008 and 2009. They graciously gave me what was theirs, and loved me unconditionally, helping me find joy in the midst of a challenging season.

Leo had a keen ability to lift me in moments of my self-doubt. "B, that's rubbish! You know you can do that." He did it in his special Leo way, and it always grounded me back into the truth of who God created me to be.

And of course, he possessed this uncanny ability to put Christ above *everything* else. My parents and I still call Leo our "modern-day Paul."

Just before I moved to South Africa in September of 2008, Leo had a seizure, caused by a tumor in his brain. Later that December, when I was living in their home, he had brain surgery. At that time in their lives, I was able to be a rock for Leo and Linda, just as they had been a rock in my life when I had arrived as a big-eyed Texan ready to launch into my "ministry plan," only to be quickly shaken out of that and into chaos. All had fallen apart and not gone according to my plan. If it wasn't for Leo and Linda O'Connor, I would have boarded a plane back to Texas after my first week in South Africa. God was shifting and stirring at lightning-speed, and I was lonely and confused. They swept me up and offered me a *home* in their house with their toddler son, Thomas. I felt part of the family immediately, and moving there gave me a great sense of comfort, peace, and security in a very trying time of my life as a stranger in a foreign land.

Just a few days after Leo's brain surgery, in his very stubborn way, he ventured out to the local supermarket with Frankenstein-esque stitches on the top of his head. I remember that Linda was so mad at him because he was exposing his wound to all sorts of germs that could negatively affect his recovery, and secondly, she was scared he would emotionally scar small children with his monster-like hairline.

Leo went to the market anyway, because he was never one to let anything stop him – not even brain surgery. He had the tenacity of a bull at times.

Watching my rock fade away into deep dependence on others, for even the most menial tasks, was a difficult thing for me. Leo struggled to show any weakness. This was not his normal way. He fought with all the strength of God He had in him, and yet, over time, the tumor ravaged his body.

Three years after I moved away from South Africa, Leo passed into eternity with Jesus. I was living outside of London at the time and was in the middle of a massive ministry outreach event to over 17,000 people. I was in charge of coordinating all the volunteers and was spinning more plates than I could handle. When I heard of Leo's death on July 12, 2012, I dropped all my plates and crumbled to pieces on the floor alongside them. The wind was knocked out of me. I couldn't move. I couldn't function. I couldn't even breathe.

My co-worker and wise friend, Elise, forced me to go home and take time away from the craziness of our event. As I often do in emotionally overwhelming times, I sat and penned a song to honor my brother, Leo:

I'll remember your ways to keep me light on my darkest days
The stories that you told never ever will grow old
I can still hear your laugh (Ha-ha), echoes in my ears and sings to my heart
I can still see you dance wooing your beautiful wife with your romance

CHORUS:

But my favorite thing about you is the way in which you loved
Christ shining from within you giving glory to God above

I'll remember you were tough, fighting to the end, never giving up

The moments that we shared etched on my heart forever to stay there
I can still hear you speak always full of life, lifting people up
I can still see you smile grinning ear-to-ear as you laugh inside

BRIDGE:

I will sing to honor you, Leo, our hero, and my friend
Christ in you, Your everything, You're forever now with Him

I recorded the song on my computer straight away and sent it to South Africa to be played at his funeral. It was my way of contributing to a day celebrating his life and legacy.

During Leo's service, which I attended virtually via my computer, the following was said: "The greater the value, the greater the loss."

It's been five years since his death, and when I reflect upon Leo, my heart still feels like a wrung-out dishtowel. It takes me back to the summer of 2012 and the following January of 2013, when we had a commemorative service for Leo at my home church in McKinney, Texas. Leo had traveled to McKinney to raise financial and prayer support for his missionary endeavors in previous years, and in so doing, impacted many lives with his charisma and passion for the gospel work he was doing among the poor in South Africa.

I stood in front of fifty people that day and told them stories about life and adventure with Leo and about how, without his friendship in my life anymore, I was in a desolate winter season:

The grief grips tight, entangling me, as if to trick me into believing it won't let go. But I know it will *eventually*. Flowers will bud. Birds will sing. Grass will paint the earth green again. Speedo stories will make me giggle with delight once more.

Leo meant so much to me, and the loss has been overwhelming.

But here's what I know. This is a winter season of my life. And though my pain is amplified, there is purpose in all this. Death has come, so that life may abound. That was Leo's desire - that through his death, others might find life in Christ.

We may never see or understand the fuller picture of life and death, but we know that after winter comes spring. That during those difficult and trying months of the bleak and cold, the empty and grey, the mystery and the mundane, through the death of seeds and plants, God has been working the soil below to blossom life and beauty all around.

My friend and brother, Leo, is like a seed. He is a seed that has died in order that life may be found.

As **John 9:1-3** reads, *"As he went along, he saw a man blind from birth. His disciples asked him, 'Rabbi, who sinned, this man or his parents, that he was born blind?' 'Neither this man nor his parents sinned,' said Jesus, 'but this happened so that the works of God might be displayed in him.'"*

The work of God has been clearly displayed in Leo's life. He faced death head-on, armed with strength and girded with the belt of unwavering faith, tenacity, and truth.

When I think about Leo, his legacy is clear. He gave everything he had and lived to serve God – the Father, Son, and Holy Spirit – with every single fiber of his being.

He loved lavishly. He gave generously. He fought tirelessly. His faith was relentless, and all this was for the sake of Christ.

I've received the intersection of Leo's life with mine as a divine gift, one that I will carry in my heart to eternity. I like to think that this man many love so dearly has not died. No, he has been birthed into a new and extravagant life of love in heaven, embraced by the welcoming arms of the Father. As he said in his last update email to his tribe of friends and family, "Your relationship with, and identity in, Jesus Christ can never be taken away from you. It is the only sure thing."

The last time I saw Leo was when I was living in Sydney, Australia. The last thing he said to me face-to-face was, "Hey B - wanna plant a church together?" That seed, his words on that day, still speak life to me because they have planted themselves deep within the soil of my heart.

I still stay in contact with Linda, who has been blessed with a new husband who also fears the Lord. I had the joy and honor of attending their wedding virtually from my computer in Texas, and they now live on the Sunshine Coast of Australia. We often text back and forth and reminisce about our time together in South Africa and about how special that season of life was. We always chat about Leo, and when my dating life comes up with Linda, she always asks, "Would Leo approve of him, B?"

That question is tattooed on my heart. As I wait for God to write my love story, in the back of my mind I know God is preparing a husband for me that would win Leo's approval.

Leo-'ello, your seed in the soil of God's hands has brought life, beautiful life. Your life has been the perfect mirror to Christ's life. Life, beautiful life. And I am blessed beyond measure to have been a small part of your story, your rock, just as you and Linda were mine.

I'm so thankful for a God who weaves lives together so seamlessly, because we need each other. We need each other on the good days and the bad days, the days of scary brain surgeries, the days when we feel lonely in a new place, the days where we need a gut-busting belly laugh, the days where we need someone to encourage our faith rather than our fear, the days where we just need someone to sit and cry with us and tell us it will all be okay in the end. We need each other, deeply, greatly, and in such profound, yet simple ways. We need each other. And I am so grateful God led me to you, Leo-'ello and Linda, the perfect picture of Christ-centered community. You inspired me deeply, encouraged me immensely, supported me firmly, and loved me unconditionally.

Your story matters for eternity, and I will carry your legacy of living life knowing that only one thing is sure - Jesus.

CHAPTER 25

Yellow Joy

"Find a place inside where there's joy, and the joy will burn out the pain."
~ Joseph Campbell

If joy was a color, it would scream yellow.

After living in South Africa for seven months, I experienced an overflow of joy in the yellowing eyes of my friend, Siyanda Mbebe. I stepped in as a Westerner wanting to do good by planting seeds of hope in her life, and walked away with seeds of hope planted deep in the soil of my own life.

Siya, as her friends called her, was a radiant, yet frail 28-year-old survivor of a tormenting disease that is still sweeping across the continent of Africa. She was HIV positive, and lived in *The Dignity House*, an around-the-clock hospice center, in the heart of balmy East London, South Africa.

I spent hours in the company of this charming yet shrinking intellect, gleaning from her the stories of a happy Xhosan tribal childhood in rural South Africa. I spent time listening to her as she mounted her soapbox about the political and socioeconomic status of her homeland, as well as her hopes and fears for its future. I heard stories of laughter and innocent childhood memories, as well as tales about the broken history of the "beautiful rainbow nation" during the struggles of the Apartheid era.

As much as I saw joy in the eyes of my friend, her words also evoked a profound sadness in my soul. I began to understand the meaning of the word tragedy. In fact, my mind raced to the overwhelming problem that we have in many parts of the United States – that of teen pregnancy. What struck me is that every time a teenage girl makes the decision to have sex with her male counterpart, she risks being infected with a sexually transmitted disease (STD) or falling pregnant, both of which can be longtime shadows. But just across the ocean in a breath-taking land of discrepancy between the rich and the poor, the white, the colored, and the black, between desolation and abundance, that same choice has life-long and potentially life-ending consequences.

Siya contracted HIV from a previous boyfriend, who neglected to tell her of his HIV positive status. She only knew that he was the carrier when she learned of his death a few years later. As a result of this, Siya only found out in 2002 that she was HIV positive. She pointed out, "You may have been living with the virus for two years because it hides itself and you don't see it immediately."

Unfortunately this is an all too common problem in South Africa. Being HIV positive carries with it an undeniable stigma and responsibility. As soon as a woman (or man) "outs" herself with HIV positive status, she becomes an outcast. Also, if she chooses to take anti-retroviral (ARV) treatment (which does not cure, but simply sustains life), she must make a commitment to continue the treatment daily for the duration of her life because as soon as the ARVs are stopped, her health takes a downward spiral for the worst, most likely resulting in death. Along with the responsibility of daily doses, there is the cost of medication (in Siya's case her treatment was provided at no cost by the *Sophumelela AIDS Clinic*) as well as the abhorrent side-effects, which can include nausea & vomiting, "pins and needles" in the legs, headaches, skin rashes, stomach discomfort, nightmares, fatigue, and diarrhea.

Therefore, many people have a fear of testing. Some would rather not know if they are HIV positive. In fact, Siya has been told that she is brave for knowing because it's easier not to know. There is too much reality and responsibility that comes with knowing.

Siya shared with me about the difficulty of her condition, "It makes people objectify me. They don't see me as a person, but as an illness. They won't touch me because they are afraid they will contract the disease. HIV is transferred from fluid to fluid, not from touch to touch, or conversation to conversation. My family sees me as a burden, and they don't take care of me. When I am lying in pain, no one will rub ointment on my feet. When I mess myself, it takes several hours before anyone notices. And even when they do, they ask, 'Why did you do this to yourself?' I feel like a burden."

As devastating as it is to feel ostracized by your own family, HIV also affects every other area of life. I vividly recall the first conversation I had with Siya about her dreams. It broke my heart, and it was all I could do to hide the tears warming in my eyes because as she shared her dreams I realized we had so much in common. She wanted to travel the world, to see the diversity of life and creation. We are women of the same age, and our shared longing in life was to love and be loved. But for Siya, she lived under the black cloud of HIV. "Will a man ever look past my status to see me for who I am? What about bearing children? Even if my body was capable, I wouldn't want to bring a sick child into this world."

There's something deeply profound about seeing people for who they are. Maybe it's because God created us to be in communion with one another, or maybe it's because it takes so much vulnerability to look beyond someone's skin color or socioeconomic status or HIV label. But for me, making that connection with Siya over the course of hours and hours spent with her for six weeks made something very clear to me. We are human. We have the capacity to love. We have the capacity to hope. We have the capacity to hurt for the hurting, to cry with the broken, to love the unlovable, to touch the untouchable, to sing with the tone-deaf, to write with the illiterate, to dance with the immobile, and to befriend the friendless. We have the capacity to see others as we were intended to see them – as human beings, to value them as God values them and to love them as Christ loves them.

Siya is my friend first. And then, and only then, she is also someone living a life ravaged by a disease that colors our world with pain, suffering, torment, abandonment, and untimely death.

And even now, separated by thousands of miles and countries and time zones, she is my friend and she has left a smile in the hollow of my heart.

Upon reflecting on God's gift of friendship in her own life, Siya said to me, "God knows that I dream of going overseas, and because this condition is impacting my possibility to do so, He has sent you to me. You've seen the world, and now you've brought the world to me."

During our last heart-wrenching hours together in South Africa, Siya gave me an incredible gift. "Bethany, I am grateful for your friendship, and I want to give you the name *Siyabonga*, which means increased gratefulness. You have come to spend time with me and have become my friend. You have seen me as a person, not as someone with a positive HIV status. Thank you."

Siya planted seeds of hope deep within my soul because she lived life with joy, despite her circumstances, and with strength, despite her weaknesses. She may very well be robbed of life at a young age by tuberculosis (TB) or pneumonia because of the impact that HIV has had on her body, but ultimately this disease will not conquer her. It will not put out that yellow beaming light of joy because in her own words Siya said, "I am not sick. I have been healed through my faith in Christ. This is just a condition that torments my body, but it does not affect my spirit. My spirit is strong. My spirit is powerful. My spirit is invincible."

I don't know about you, but I want her yellow joy.

* When I left South Africa in 2009, I honestly felt like I might never see Siya again. Since then, God has miraculously given her renewed health and she now works to help those across South Africa who are more in need than she is. In her latest communication with me she said, "I had very remarkable moments – you treated me as a princess. I thank God for your life. You loved me genuinely, my friend, regardless of the circumstances and state I was in. God places the right people at the right time. Thank you, my friend."

CHAPTER 26

From Under the Veil of Chaos

"God takes everyone he loves through a desert. It is his cure for our wandering hearts." ~ Paul Miller

Whenever I'm in the rich, tangible Presence of God, I feel like nothing, like absolute zilch. And it's because I know that without Him, I *am* nothing.

Perhaps that sounds like a harsh, sadistic view of life. But if God wasn't at the helm, I would've jumped ship years ago.

I arrived my first day at Hillsong International Leadership College in Sydney, Australia, with a straight-edged confidence that I later learned was, unfortunately, translated as arrogance. What I thought to be the launching pad for an already confident woman of God turned out to be two grueling years of Bethany in pieces, scattered on the floor, trampled by the heaviness of one humbling moment after another.

It is only in hindsight that I see that God's plans for my time at Bible College were opportunity and positioning, yes, but more importantly they were about the humbling of my heart, while teaching me the work and surrender of a true servant.

Admittedly this is not something I've accomplished yet, and something that I probably never will. But I have a new and greater understanding of God's goodness in seasons of brokenness. I have a fresh revelation of the fact that if I am in His way, He can't actually use me effectively.

I heard it preached countless times from the Hillsong platform that the experience of Bible college would commence a difficult journey from "I can do this myself" to "I can't do this at all" to "I am compelled to do this *because* God is with me."

My pilgrimage during my time at Hillsong turned out to be exactly that. I came to Australia, having already spent several years doing ministry in France, Switzerland, and South Africa. My glory years of ministry were in Europe. I was there to love and serve international students and au pairs, but as is the nature of much ministry work, I was the one receiving love and blessings. Our focus was relational evangelism – building strong relationships with people, meeting them where they were, and out of the natural overflow of connection, sharing the truth of the gospel with them. As a result, I spent my days meeting with au pairs, snowboarding with them on the weekends, and counseling them through hard times. In addition, I got to lead out-of-the-box worship sets at my international church and endlessly tour the European continent on holidays. There were some difficult days in the mix as well, but overall life was good and God was moving.

Ministry in South Africa was the opposite. I was confronted with hardships I'd never encountered before both personally and in the stories and faces of many I met. Life was hard for many people there, and the political and cultural climate was rife with uncertainty and fear about the future. Along with that, I was serving orphans, HIV and AIDS patients, and walking alongside friends as they watched a very unwelcome brain tumor radically impact their lives. That was one of the desert seasons of my life, but God always shows up in those hard, dry places as well. I was about to learn that *again*

With an array of ministry experience under my belt, I arrived in Australia with ammunition that pelted people with my credentials as an international missionary and God-chaser. At first, I spouted-off my stories and tales of adventure and faith like a gushing Italian fountain. Slowly over time, though, I got tired of talking about myself. I became exhausted with the constant self-promotion just to be accepted and viewed as special by my fellow God-chasing friends.

It's harsh when God removes the self-soothing mechanisms in our lives, when He takes the cucumbers off our eyelids so that we can see the truth about ourselves.

I'm not sure the exact moment that sent me crashing to the ground, but I was suddenly acutely aware that I was doing God's work, in part, as a benefit for *myself*, not for His kingdom. In fact, the more scarring reality was that I was possibly hurting more people than helping them along the way.

I know God is a God of redemption, and I do not for one second believe that my mistakes can undermine His sovereignty. I'm simply asserting that my pride was getting in the way of truly seeing and loving people as He sees and loves them.

One Tuesday morning, in the middle of chapel worship, I took an honest snapshot of my life and confessed to God that I had been living as a very prideful, arrogant person who wanted things done my way, on my terms. I realized that I was selfish and self-serving, pursuing the things of God more as a benefit to my own life rather than the lives of others. So essentially, I was missing the whole point.

After this confession, I was violently shot into a cycle of total disbelief. *I cannot do this. I am too broken to be used by God. My thoughts are wayward, self-seeking, and judgmental. I am sinful. Who do I think I am? I don't have the capacity it takes to live full-speed for God. I'll never be worthy.*

These thoughts pressed on my heart daily, and I began walking under the fog of doubt, self-hatred, self-condemnation, and confusion.

This overarching crisis of "self" continued through to my last semester at Hillsong in 2011. I was sitting in my preaching class under the brilliance of Robert Fergusson, one of the church's greatest communicators. We were discussing the idea that, oftentimes in the desert seasons of our lives, nothing turns up but God. I suddenly saw the progression of my life's journey, ripe with one desert season after another, as God-ordained and necessary for me to be wholly intimate with Him, resulting in total surrender to His purposes.

In that class, from under the veil of inner turmoil and chaos, the light of grace emerged perfectly and gloriously and brought new purpose and meaning to my life. The desert seasons have resulted in deeper faith and closer intimacy with the God of the universe, so that, hopefully, my life will bless others and point to Him.

Unfortunately, I think it's easy and not uncommon when you grow up in the church your whole life to grapple with the real concept of grace. There's always the temptation to think that because you've never really done anything that you would define as "terrible," you are good enough to merit God's favor. This is not something we readily admit. We think we are good people, and we deserve God's love because we have always been well-behaved, steering clear of the seven deadly sins.

Yet, in that chapel moment, when I looked upon the snapshot of my life with God-eyes, I was so revolted with my selfishness and arrogance that it made me sick to my stomach. Revelation 3:16 became very real and very poignant, *"So, because you are lukewarm - neither hot nor cold - I am about to spit you out of my mouth."* The Greek word for spit is *emeō*, which literally translates, "to vomit or throw-up."

In January of 2011, my alma mater, Baylor University, had been invited to participate in a football bowl game for the first time in sixteen years. My whole green-and-gold family was elated about this event, and because I was home for the holidays from overseas, I went down to Houston a couple of days early to spend the weekend with my aunt.

I'm not sure if it was the Tex-Mex I inhaled or the ice cream sundae that followed, but I was overtaken by the demon of food poisoning. That first night, I lay awake in a strange bed, barely able to move six feet to the nearest toilet, shaking, and miserable.

Once I finally managed to drag myself to the toilet, stopping along the way to relieve my burning face on the cool tile, I mustered up the strength to hover over the toilet, and threw-up. Violence. Abuse. My body was convulsing in literal gut-wrenching pain.

Well, we all know how it goes when you vomit. I honestly consider it my least favorite thing in the entire world. I would rather wear clothespins as earrings than repeatedly retch into a toilet basin.

Unfortunately, though, I did repeat this act about eight times over the course of the next four hours.

As if my twisted stomach wasn't enough, the jalapeño spices from my dinner had made their way into my sinuses. I can literally say I've never been so uncomfortable in all of my life. At one point, it felt like the base of my brain was actually burning. I couldn't sleep because I thought my head was going to combust and rain a fountain of jalapeño juice.

When I saw my sin and my brokenness with God's eyes that day in chapel, I actually *wanted* to vomit because I wanted to rid myself of the pride and selfishness that was poisoning and incapacitating me for the purposes of God.

In the middle of my spiritual retching, God put the cool and soothing cloth of His grace over my face and wiped my tears away.

I live under the banner of thankfulness for His favor on my life, for His protection from so many things, situations, and relationships that could've brought total damage and devastation to my heart. I am acutely aware of His grace. I am acutely aware that I need Him, that my life is and has never been about being good, about doing the things I thought were right. But my life has forever been and always will be a testament to His grace and His mercy, on this my feeble, human life.

Reflecting back on this progression of confidence in my life, my crisis moment in Bible College dipped me into the pit of "I can't" because I am not humanly capable, but His grace has brought me to a point of resolve. "I can" because He has created me for a purpose, and by His strength "I *must*" live in obedience to things He has asked of me, so that others may be blessed and He may be glorified.

So regardless of your past, regardless of your own wayward thoughts, God wants to redeem your brokenness and use you. But first He wants to move you from the belief that you can do life on your own, that you can do everything in your own strength, just the way you like it.

On the way to the Promised Land, He may just want to take you by way of the valley, into the deepest, driest desert, where He wants to show you that when everything around you seems dead and lifeless in a place where nothing goes right and nothing turns up, He is *always* right and He *always* turns up. In fact, I heard it said once that your desert season - your personal wilderness – is the safest place because it's where you are confronted with only the necessary, God.

As you exit that desert, though perhaps a little tired and sore, you will emerge with new eyes and a greater strength. You will walk with purpose towards your destiny. You will walk with joy, because He has been with you through it all. You will walk in freedom, because you realize that He is at work within you and wants to do amazing things through you.

God, the great Artist of breath and life, is living inside of me and He's living inside of you. I can do what He's asking me to do, and so can you. We can. We must because He is doing it through us, and there are a lot of people on the other side of our obedience. Many are waiting to be seen and loved by people who see and love with the eyes of God.

CHAPTER 27

Four Postcards

"For since the creation of the world God's invisible qualities—his eternal power and divine nature—have been clearly seen, being understood from what has been made, so that people are without excuse."
~ Romans 1:20 (NIV)

Homesickness is not something familiar to me. It's not that I don't miss my family and friends, or that I don't miss iced tea and the scintillating pairing of chips and queso. I absolutely miss people, and undeniably I miss the tastes of Texas. It's just that I am usually on the go, and therefore, I don't have time to stop and sulk about the things that I want, but can't have.

So when homesickness fell on me one night like a fever slaps a red-cheeked kid across the face, I was taken aback. I remember that I was sitting on my black and white polka-dotted bed, looking out the window on a rainy Australian spring night. I'm sure I was supposed to be working on an assessment or writing a song for class, but I was unexpectedly crippled by a desire to be anywhere but on that bed pondering my life through my dirty windowpane.

In a dramatic gesture, I sighed out sadness and boredom and turned my head to the left, where four distinct postcards, taped on my otherwise drab wall, captured my attention.

There was a picture of the Eiffel Tower surrounded by blossoming pink flowers, the image of a giant patriotic Texas Lone Star, a postcard that boasted the beauty of the snow-covered Swiss Matterhorn, and a romantic landscape of Table Mountain in Cape Town.

As my gaze fell upon this collage of postcards dotting my wall, my gears began spinning and I was suddenly reliving special moments from the places each postcard represented. See, the unique thing about these cards is that each one reminded me of the season of life I spent in that particular place.

And because I was already swimming in a sea of homesickness, this piercing nostalgia penetrated my emotions and pinned my heart to the wall. I started reflecting on my life and started convincing myself that I never actually lived in these places, that these postcards represented figments of my imagination, not the real journey of my life. I was thrown into a dark pit of confusion and told myself that I never walked Parisian streets savoring warm *pain au chocolat* or biked around the *Arche de Triomphe* with my best friend. Surely, I never snowboarded a path through fresh fields of powder or spent my weekends hiking and paragliding with au pairs in Interlaken. A baby seal never jumped in front of my surfboard while riding a wave and I never witnessed a fiery golden South African Easter sunrise. I never tickled my toes in the crystal blue waters of Lake Powell near the Grand Canyon or climbed hay bales in front of an audience of curious Texas longhorns.

As I let this confusion overtake me, I sat punctured before God. I listened to the stillness of silence. My head was pounding and my heart was numb, and this journey of remembrance had left me writhing in emotional pain.

And then I heard the calm, but booming voice of God.

"Bethany, what do all these postcards have in common?"

I don't know. What? I wasn't really up for this game. I graduated elementary school a long time ago with a cute colorful diploma and a box of shiny crayons in hand. Honestly, I was in no mood for this kind of question and was feeling really tender and homesick for my life in other places.

The question rang again, "Bethany, what do all these postcards have in common?"

I've learned something very important about my relationship with God: when He asks, I answer. Because if I don't, He usually keeps asking until I do. So, with a very selfish motive to expedite this conversation with the least amount of grueling truth that may be revealed, I turned my head back towards the postcards and began studying them intently. (Can you tell I was not in a good place emotionally?)

It wasn't long before my eyes were drawn to the similarity between the four postcards. They had something striking in common. The main symbol or image on each card was pointing upward. The Eiffel Tower towers upward. The top tip of the Texas Star shoots upward. The Matterhorn reaches skyward. The mountains, surrounding Table Mountain, point heavenwards.

As I was mulling over these strange parallels, I grabbed my journal and penned the following words above a colored-pen sketch of all these significant landmarks:

These deeply nostalgic symbols and landmarks point UPWARD, as if God is saying, "Remember Me? I am the reason all of this beauty is here. I AM here. And EVERYWHERE you go, there will I be."

I would like to say that in that moment, my homesickness dissipated, but the truth is, it grew. This time, though, I was homesick for the glory of God. I was so humbled and jubilant, like I was floating on the sea of His love.

I didn't just live in France driving two little Cambodian girls to school daily; I did so with divine purpose. I didn't just live in Switzerland spending every waking moment with lonely au pairs; I did so with divine purpose. I didn't just hold the hands of orphans and pray with my frail HIV-ridden friend, I did so with divine purpose. I didn't just grow up on a quiet hill in Texas in middle-class America; I did so with divine purpose. I didn't just lead worship at a small international church in Switzerland; I did so with divine purpose. I didn't just lead a connect group of eighteen to twenty-five year olds in Sydney, I did so with divine purpose. I didn't just paint an African collage for my friend's non-believing parents; I did so with divine purpose. I didn't just write a song for a friend having a tough day; I did so with divine purpose.

Out of despair that rainy Australian spring day emerged a blossom of passion and fervor for a God that not only loves me, for a God that not only blesses me, for a God that not only sees me, but for a God that is always with me and who promises in His Word to "never leave me, nor forsake me." (Hebrews 13:5)

Sometimes I wonder how we can miss the obvious so easily. How is it that our God has created things to grow upward and we build things that reach skyward, and yet we miss His message that whispers so simply, "Remember Me?"

I'm calling myself out on the rug here and declaring that I want to remember Him. I want to see Him. I want to know Him. Because He knows me, and everything I do by His generous grace and orchestration, is with divine, kingdom purpose. So, just like the Eiffel Tower, the Texas Lone Star, the Matterhorn, and the Cape Town mountains burst upward and skyward, I, too, want my life to burst upward and shout and scream, "I remember You! I remember You! To God be the glory!"

Chapter 28

You Are Beautiful

"Blessed are they who see beautiful things in humble places where other people see nothing." ~ Camille Pissarro

On a lovely November spring day when I was studying at Bible College in Australia, I decided to venture out to the world-famous Bondi beach. I boarded my first bus, and as I watched the blur of trees, cars and people passing by, I invited God to join me in my day. I prayed a little prayer on the hard seat of the bus that went something like this: "Jesus, open my eyes to see as You see today. Open my heart to love as You love today."

Moments later, lifting my nose out of my book, I glanced up and noticed that a young woman with severe disabilities was boarding the bus by its ramp. She was riding in style in a motorized wheelchair, decorated with a plethora of shopping bags and piles of personal stuff. In fact, it looked like she might be going on a trip.

I looked at her and considered the difficulty that each day must bring, and as tears started welling-up in my eyes for this woman's plight, I noticed that she had a dazzling smile on her face. She was exuding joy, happiness and enthusiasm, despite her physical limitations.

And then the whisper of God broke my meditation. He sweetly said, "Tell her she's beautiful."

Thoughts exploded in my head like sizzling popcorn. *What? Who am I? I can't do that. That's weird. She'll think I'm weird. The people on the bus will point and stare and wonder. No, I can't and I won't.*

Battling God's voice thumping in my heart, my train of thought shifted to, "I *did* invite the Holy Spirit into my day." So, I mustered enough strength to decide that *if* I was going to say anything, I should say something more like, "God loves you."

I distinctly remember that God interrupted my analysis, "Stop overanalyzing. Just tell her she's beautiful."

I continued to squirm in my seat, pondering when and how I would actually act in obedience. I knew I couldn't escape God's instruction to speak to this woman, and so with sweat beading on my forehead and fingers twitching from nervousness, I finally collected the courage to boldly speak to her on God's behalf.

As my bus stop approached, I grabbed my bag and walked towards this woman near the front of the bus, stopping directly in front of her. I bent down, gently resting my hand on hers, as I looked into her eyes with a warm smile and said, "I think you're beautiful."

I didn't stay in front of her long enough to see her reaction because it's all I could do to dam the flood of tears welling in my eyes. So I quickly hopped off the bus, and headed to my train. As I did, I thanked God for His extravagant love, and for using me to pour His love onto a stranger.

That's the thing about God. He *wants* us to pour His extravagant love on others. In fact, isn't that the whole point of our faith? We are blessed so that others will be blessed. We are loved so that others will be loved. And all of this is rooted in the deep, merciful, love of Christ. We are agents of change that speak life and hope and grace over a world that is messy and broken and disheveled.

I am struck by the fact that in the moment of hearing God's voice on the bus that day, my audacious retort to Him promoted what message I should convey to her instead of what He had clearly told me to say. I wonder why I thought it was more important that she knew God loved her more than her knowing she was beautiful.

I don't know the answer to that, because obviously it's important she knows that God is the source of love, and that she's created just as she is for a purpose, and that God doesn't make mistakes. In fact, there are a lot of things that I could've told her that day that might have been just as important, if not more important, than telling her she was beautiful.

But here's what I know of God from my personal experience in the way He gently works with me. *He always meets me where I am.*

When I am sad, He embraces me and says, "You're not alone." When I'm broken, He whispers, "I will make you whole again." When I feel that no one values me, He tells me, "I created you for a purpose." When I am overwhelmed because life feels chaotic, He reminds me, "I am a God of order." When I feel inadequate to the task He's calling me to, He says, "My grace is sufficient for you." When I feel like I'm drowning and cannot go on, He whispers, "My strength is made perfect in weakness." When I feel discarded by the world because I'm still single in my mid-thirties, He gazes into my eyes and says, "You are beautiful, cherished, and chosen."

I don't know what the lady in that wheelchair needed that day. I don't have words that heal, but God does. I don't have words that change lives, but God does. I don't have the right words, but He *always* does.

He knew exactly what she needed to hear that day, and I was so humbled and grateful to be a small part of sharing His life-giving words with her. My prayer is that my eyes and ears would always be open to seeing and hearing Him. Not for myself, but so that others may know the good, good love of our Father God.

CHAPTER 29

Hummingbirds & Kittens

"In the depth of winter I finally learned that there was in me an invincible summer." ~ *Albert Camus*

I found a dead hummingbird once on a walk in the morning sun. Its feet were tucked quietly under its belly and the green iridescence of its top feathers was still shimmering. And I cried. I cried because something beautiful was dead.

Death strikes the chord of grief. It marshals in feelings of loss, hopelessness, despair, and darkness. It confronts the living.

One of the most profound lessons I learned when I lived in Australia is that sometimes we must allow things to die, so that God can resurrect them and breathe new life back into them in His timing. We must allow ourselves to experience the darkness of those seasons, so that we can fully embrace the light.

I would be absolutely heart-happy if I were to walk outside and find that same beautiful hummingbird buzzing around me. I'm not saying God is going to bring this bird back to life, although He could. What I am saying, though, is that I *know* that God takes the dreams in our lives and lets them die for a season, so that when the timing is right, they will be resurrected alongside their stronger, wiser, more trusting dreamers.

Oddly enough, this pain of death is oftentimes disguised as the pain of birthing something new.

I heard a story once about a family who went to pick a batch of wild mushrooms and then invited their friends for a feast. After dinner, as they were cleaning up, they fed some leftovers to their cat.

A little while later, the cat started foaming at the mouth and rolling around on the floor, groaning in pain. The family immediately took action and called their doctor, in fear that they had just ingested poisonous mushrooms. They rushed to the hospital and had their stomachs pumped. They called their friends to do the same. It was only upon returning home several hours later that they were greeted by their happy cat and its litter of newborn kittens.

The cat was experiencing *birthing pains*, not dying pains. When I think of my life and the dreams that God has planted in my heart, what I realize is that sometimes I have to let those dreams die. That death is not actual death, though. It's laying something at the feet of Jesus, so that in His Sovereignty, in His timing, He can breathe new life again and usher-forth new birth.

I lived in Geneva, Switzerland for several years working with a ministry to international students and au pairs. One of our partner ministries hosted a Prayer Labyrinth in the Old Town one evening, and during my time of prayer and meditation, I was encouraged to light a candle to pray for someone's salvation. I chose an old friend who has been chasing darkness his whole life. As I stood there in prayerful reflection, the flame symbolized two things for me: 1) God breathing new life into him, and 2) my role in helping to spread Christ's light to this friend. I was overcome with such a burden to pray for him, and at that very moment, a baby started crying loudly outside the window of the antiquated church hall where I stood. To me, that symbolized the pain of a new birth – living in the darkness before being birthed into the light.

Donald Miller says in *Blue Like Jazz,* "Sometimes the path of joy winds through a dark valley."

I know this to be true in my own life. The darker the season, the brighter the light and joy feels at the end. Sometimes the darkness *is* the death that we feel. It is the place where all our hopes and dreams have gone to die. Darkness is the graveyard for the way we saw our lives panning-out, the way we wanted things to workout. It's the hopelessness I feel, as a single woman in her mid-thirties, that life has passed me by because all my friends have been married for over a decade now and are finished having children. It's the hopelessness you feel when you've been fired from the job you love because of a huge misunderstanding. It's the hopelessness I feel when I feel misunderstood by almost everyone I know. It's the hopelessness you feel when you move your family across the country for your husband's job, and everything in you is screaming because it's the last thing you want to do. It's the hopelessness I feel in thinking that my life isn't where I thought it would be by this point. It's the hopelessness you feel when you've lost a child, a close friend, or a family member who has suffered greatly.

But walking that path of hopelessness and despair leads you straight to the Creator. His seasons have purpose, and therefore, so do ours. The natural rhythm of God's seasons teaches us much about the rhythm of our personal and spiritual lives. Before every spring, there is winter. It is the beautiful way of God's created order for nature and for our lives.

I'm currently sitting here on a February day in north Texas. Typically this time of year is bitter, cold, and gloomy. My mother's birthday falls during the first week of February, and she's spent many years wishing she had anything but a February birthday. In fact, I always tell her she needs to move to the southern hemisphere to actually enjoy the weather on her birthday. In 2015, we were completely iced-in for five days. Stores were closed, roads were impassible, and people sat bundled-up in their homes catching an itchy case of cabin fever.

But this year is different. It's 70°F outside, and it's projected to be 80°F degrees this coming weekend.

As beautiful and refreshing as it is, there's something that doesn't feel *right*. It's like the normal rhythm of the seasons is completely off. Without winter, how can we enjoy spring and summer? Without days full of dreary gloom and darkness, how can we fully embrace those days full of sunshine and light? Without death, how can we know life?

For me, I'd actually rather skip winter. I'm thrilled by new things budding to life in spring, and by the fullness of joy and sustenance in summer. I love the final bursts of color on leaves in autumn, but I want to run screaming and crying away from the cold, hard, dead ground of winter. But I also know that winter is necessary. It is spiritually proven that things must die in order for new things to come to life.

Winter always reminds me of death and darkness before new life comes. I find it to be such a mystical season of the year; the trees wear the face of mourners and the ground is blanched and bare. Have you ever considered what's happening beneath the surface, though? Have you ever wondered what's beyond what your eyes can see?

When I walk along barren streets, I think about the magic of creation that is happening right below the surface of my footsteps and in the trees that express sadness and death on the outside. I imagine that there are all sorts of colors popping and fizzing into existence at that very moment. I imagine new life being weaved together beneath the driest bark and the coldest ground. I imagine that there is a divine party raging below the surface. No eye can see this, other than the host of the party, our Creator.

When I'm in seasons of dryness, doubt, discouragement or death, I like to picture that the same wild party is happening underneath the surface of my own heart and mind. God is exploding colors within me to create new life and fresh dreams, and He is breathing life into the old, seemingly dead things. So that, when spring eases in and winter fades away, those dreams will blossom like Texas wildflowers, inspiring me with bold colors and floral scents. I will remember that every spring requires a winter, and that hopelessness and darkness is always replaced by His hope and light. I will remember that death is necessary for new things to come to life. I will remember that, despite her pain, the cat wasn't dying. She was giving birth to something new and glorious!

CHAPTER 30

More Than a Haircut

"If I continue to endure, I will conquer." ~ Winston Churchill

I think most people would say they've had a bad haircut at some point in their life. This would be true for myself on more than one occasion, but until July of 2010, I had never had a haircut that carried with it so much personal and spiritual weight.

Singleness comes with its battles. I have always been a very independent person, and yet I have always desired to be dependent on someone other than myself. My parents have played this role for the bulk of my life, even well into my adulthood, supporting and empowering a lifestyle that has gone against the typical Texas grain.

Beyond empowerment and support, I desire to be intimately known by a man, and to journey life together in love and partnership. I desire to meet a man who is so deeply in love with God that I have to run in all-out abandon to keep up with his pace of faith.

I've always been wired to do things uniquely, with my own Bethany-flair, whether in dress or hair color, choice or opinion, I've learned how to be confident in who God created me to be. By His grace, I have been protected from so many situations that could've resulted in emotional disasters and total breakdowns.

All that to say, if I could pinpoint the one cyclical pattern of struggle in my life, the "thorn in my flesh," it would fall under the category entitled, "matters of the heart."

As I write this, I am in my mid-thirties, and have had very few real relationships. In fact, my first official relationship with potential came about in 2013. My problem hasn't necessarily been with a lack of prospects. My biggest battle has been a debilitating disease - an *obsession* with the *ideal*.

I'm a dreamer. I'm an idealist. So when it comes to men in my life, I have really astronomical expectations. Not because I have a grocery list of non-negotiable desires like must love to laugh, must snowboard, must dress hipster, must have brown hair, and must sing like an angel. All these things might be a bonus but it's actually because I cling to the belief that God wants the most God-honoring, spiritual leader for my life.

This isn't a bad thing in and of itself. It's just that it can be tricky to navigate the cultural norms of life when this level of idealism is the filter through which all men must pass with flying colors.

In July 2010, I was living in Australia and had my hair cut by a guy I knew. The hands that held the scissors that stripped me of my long, blonde locks were the same hands that had bruised my heart over the previous nine months.

My hairdresser (we'll call him Red) and I had met in an "only God could orchestrate this" kind of way the previous November over the phone, while I was making recruiting calls for my leadership college. We had such an immediate connection during that first phone call and even had friends in common. After getting to know him a bit more, he *did* answer to all those ideals on my "non-existent" list of things I desire in a man, but most importantly, he seemed to fit the role of a God-honoring, spiritual leader.

As has been my pattern in the past, my heart took off and my brain couldn't catch-up. I constantly preached to myself, "Don't go there mentally. You don't even know him. Let God orchestrate things naturally." But it's as if my heart was completely deaf and dumb to these warnings.

Then, of course, the ugly pattern of taking something I've received as a gift from God and manipulating it for my selfish purposes reared its very ugly, grotesque head. So even though I knew exactly what *not* to do in regards to this new interest, I did it anyway. That reminds me of what Paul says in Romans 7:15-21:

I do not understand what I do. For what I want to do I do not do, but what I hate I do. And if I do what I do not want to do, I agree that the law is good. As it is, it is no longer I myself who do it, but it is sin living in me. For I know that good itself does not dwell in me, that is, in my sinful nature. For I have the desire to do what is good, but I cannot carry it out. For I do not do the good I want to do, but the evil I do not want to do—this I keep on doing. Now if I do what I do not want to do, it is no longer I who do it, but it is sin living in me that does it. So I find this law at work: Although I want to do good, evil is right there with me.

I'm all-too-good at hearing what I want to hear and fabricating a reality in my mind. This instantly included Red as my husband and the two of us traveling the globe preaching and leading worship to thousands of people. Of course, as this false reality in my head settled into the roots of my heart, along came three beautiful children frolicking in the luscious, green grass that bordered our colorful, happy home. And on it went– this emotionally detrimental cycle of the "what ifs" and "what will bes" in my life.

This contrived non-reality and the dreams of a life together with Red entangled my heart and suffocated my faith. In fact, it wrapped its arms so tightly around me that I all I could see was the prospect of Red and nothing else. I held it so close to my heart that I was blinded by anything, let alone anyone else - even God.

Fast-forward nine months past all the emotional grit and grime of miscommunication and misunderstanding between Red and me to a life-altering moment in my kitchen. I sat on a barstool twiddling my thumbs in nervous anticipation of a shoulder-length mod-cut, which was going to be a pretty big change from my golden "hippie" locks.

Without a mirror nearby, I watched long strands of hair fall to the kitchen floor in front of me, making my heart thump in nervousness. Something felt off in that moment. The world seemed to be spinning on a different axis and chunks of my hair were going with it. Despite all this, nothing could've prepared me for what I saw when I finally looked into the mirror.

I stood up to see my new haircut. Horror struck! My long, blonde hair had morphed into a short, brown, boyish pixie cut.

With a fake smile plastered across my face in an effort to disguise my disgust, I squeaked out a high-pitched, "I love it!"

The haircut itself wasn't actually bad. The problem was that behind my pseudo-smile, I knew all my confidence and femininity had been swept up and thrown into the trashcan along with my blonde locks of hair.

I soothed my shock by telling myself, "It's only hair. It will grow back." But these words were only a Band-Aid. There was a much deeper wound festering beneath the surface that needed divine intervention and healing. The haircut lit the wick that led to an internal dynamite explosion of insecurity, shame, and darkness.

Over the next six months of my life, God used this explosion to dig deep into the crevices of my heart, exposing my idolatry of self and my unbalanced focus on finding a husband. In my time at Bible college, I was learning so much about taking my thoughts captive and allowing God to realign my heart with His. This was my darkest season while in Australia, because God allowed me to hit rock bottom, and in doing so, He smashed my misaligned identities and ripped away every security net beneath me.

One particular day in late October, in an attempt to lull myself away from the pain of these new revelations about my selfishness and idolatrous desires, I pulled out my paints to express the darkness I felt within. When I put my brush to the canvas, I had this vision, and proceeded to paint what I saw. I sketched the outline of a girl with her left arm outstretched forward, tightly gripping a giant heart that was casting colors of light in every direction. This girl had her eyes closed, a pensive expression on her face, as if to say this action of extending the heart out had cost her something. It weighed heavily on her like a burden. She held her head turned slightly over her right shoulder, and had a very distinct hairstyle. She had brown cropped, blunt bangs and edgy pieces around her ears, with the length falling in the back to midway between below the chin and just-above-the-shoulder.

I didn't think much of this piece when I painted it, other than it served its purpose of taking my mind off my own hated haircut, and therefore had provided me solace. When I was finished painting, I left the canvas lying on my wooden desk to dry.

The next day I inspected my artwork to see if it was dry so that I could hang it on my wall. When I reached over to touch the painting, I realized that it was wet and dripping with some odd substance. I investigated the neighboring items on my desk, and realized that the oil jar holding my fragrance sticks had been knocked over. When I surveyed my desk, I saw that the only place the oil had spilled was on my painting. It didn't hit the desk. It didn't touch my pile of papers nearby. It *only* covered my painting.

Because of the oil, the painting had this unearthly glow about it. In that moment, I knew that God was speaking to me. The painting had been anointed.

I pondered this and heard the voice of Love. God gently pressed on my heart and said, "Bethany, when your hair looks like the girl's in this picture, your heart will be healed and whole. You will be strong and victorious. Take this outer transformation as a divine sign of the work that I'm doing on the inside of your heart."

At that, I crumpled up into a heap on the floor.

I sobbed and sobbed, because I knew that there was purpose in this dark season. I knew that God had intervened in my life because He wanted to show me that He is the only one that fills the empty spaces in my heart. That He is the first Love of my life. He is the *only* Love. That He is the great healer of wounded hearts and broken messes. He is the restorer of identities and calling and purpose. And that He works for the good of those who love Him.

He also wanted to teach me that my confidence and security was not and could not be in the way I looked. It wasn't found in the way my hair was styled, cut, or colored. My confidence and security, femininity and uniqueness, were only to be found *in* Him.

For the next several months, I kept that painting on my wall as a reminder of God's good purpose in my life. It reminded me that I would eventually emerge out the other end stronger and more secure as the Bethany He actually created me to be.

The days didn't get any easier from there. In fact, there were many days that I had to talk myself out of running down to the local pharmacy to buy blonde hair dye just to make it bearable to look at myself in the mirror. But every time I was tempted to cover up my pain with a touch of blonde, I was reminded that God was working diligently and gently to bring out the real me that had been hidden. I was still Bethany. I just wasn't the blonde version of myself. And that had to be all right because there was divine purpose in it.

What I love about God is that He doesn't ask us to do something that He hasn't already given us the strength to do. He knew that in that season, I would need an extra dose of time and space to reflect and allow Him to realign and mend my wayward, idolatrous heart.

In that very season – the one I would call my "dark" season – He spoke the most beautiful and redemptive instruction to my heart. He asked me to paint. And He gave me time to paint. And you see, with God, it all comes full-circle. This haircut, which I thought had ruined my life and stripped away my confidence and femininity, was redeemed and given new purpose through a measly painting I crafted one gloomy afternoon. I didn't realize at the time that the colors dancing off the tip of my paintbrush would form an image that would come to mean so much to me. I didn't realize that God could take the emotions of such a tough season and use them to produce some of the most inspired and magnetizing paintings I had ever created. Never before had I allowed so much of myself to sprinkle alongside paint onto a canvas. But in this season of death and darkness, some of my most poignant pieces arose.

These pieces were never for me, though. I always just painted how I felt, but there were unforgettable moments where I saw my friends impacted by my work. After staring at a certain piece on my wall, one friend in particular, cried a river of tears because God was stirring her heart. The color and tangible emotion that came forth from my own personal dark season had reached into her soul and connected with her own story. It was affirming her journey from darkness into light, despair into freedom.

What I learned from God about my life is that He can take the seemingly ordinary things in our lives – an unexpected haircut or simple painting – and breathe His life new and afresh, so that we begin to see things as He sees them.

Eight months after my pixie cut, I looked into the mirror, and in a quick instance, realized that my hair matched the girl's in the painting. It had made the journey, which meant *I* had made the journey. I reflected back and saw that the transformation God had done in my heart, though painful at times, had happened seamlessly and relatively quickly.

I kept my brunette hair for many years after that as a reminder of

God's goodness and faithfulness. Broken hearts heal. Hair grows back.

Chapter 31

Paint with God

"The more we let God take us over, the more truly ourselves we become because He made us."~ C.S. Lewis

When I lived in Australia, painting became my safe place. It was an excuse to create like the Creator.

I love to paint. There's something therapeutic about splashing vivid colors onto a snow-white canvas and watching beauty morph before me. You see, I have this fascination with transformation. I find inspiration in observing or partaking in visible change. That's why painting is such a treasure to me.

This tool that soothes my soul has brought revelation to my life in recent days. My approach to painting speaks volumes about the way I want to live my life.

My routine is this: I start with a blank canvas. I clear a table and lay the canvas on top of old newspaper. Then I gather my paintbrushes, my box of acrylic paints, and my paint palette, which is usually smeared with a smorgasbord of dried paint from my previous creative sessions. I make sure I have a full roll of paper towels nearby and then I find an old cup and fill it with water, placing it on the table next to my paint palette. I scroll through my music selection and pick something that suits my mood, and turn the volume up to drown out any other noise around me. Only then am I ready to paint.

I pick a paintbrush from my collection of about fifty, and I start squeezing random paint colors onto the palette. I dip my brush, and I race away into a world where color is endless and where time seems to stand still.

I don't wait on my muse. I don't wait until I can see what's ahead.

I don't wait until it feels right. I don't wait until I know exactly what's going to happen. I don't wait until something moves me.

I just paint.

I don't take my pencil and sketch things out first. I don't sit and dream first. I don't mark things with a ruler. I don't map things out. I don't draw guidelines to keep my angles straight.

I just paint.

I don't stop to analyze things. I don't wonder why things aren't panning out as I thought they might. I don't focus on what's not in the painting. I don't dwell on how it could look different.

I just paint.

When I make a mistake, I don't fret. I don't toss my canvas aside and call it ugly. I focus on fixing the mishap. I add more paint to my brush and work with the mistake to shape it into something new.

Then, I paint more.

I am patient with the colors on the canvas before me. I take my brush and use it to swipe color, building texture, layer, and depth until the mistake has been completely redeemed.

Then I continue to paint because the creative process of starting with something that looks like nothing and ending up with something I've created thrills me. I am invigorated by the organic unfolding of life and beauty before my eyes as I paint. My brush is simply the tool in my fingers. I am the artist. I am actively creating. When I create, I feel the most alive.

There's an electric coupling that happens in that moment.

When I'm painting, I feel the colors. I feel them dabbing around on the canvas, I feel them bringing life to dull surfaces. I feel them telling a story. I feel them connecting with other colors to form new colors. I feel their bond. I feel the merging of colors with different uses to form new colors with new uses.

I just paint.

My favorite part of the painting journey is that as I paint, I watch the colors and lines take shape. I watch them emerge from nothingness into something-ness. When I'm finished with the painting, I sit back and gaze with wonder upon what has materialized. I take a deep breath and marvel at the creation.

I want my life to be like that.

Quite often I struggle to get out of my head. I can't seem to move past the things I don't have, or the way that life isn't panning out how I thought it might. I get bogged down in analyzing everything that's happening. I ask *why* repeatedly like a broken record. I tell myself that if I will just sit and dream and wait on my muse, it will all come. And more than that, it will all come just like I've expected that it will.

But life is never like that. Life never pans out how we thought it would.

That's because life is organic, ever evolving, always changing.

I had a conversation once that struck me as an artist. I was about to embark on a new ministry adventure in yet another country, but this opportunity was shrouded with lots of loose ends, unknowns, and initial challenges. As I was chatting through my fears with my close friend, Kerstin, she said, "Bethany, choose to see this opportunity as a blank canvas. It's great if God hands you a piece of art, but it's even greater if He hands you a blank canvas and asks you to paint *with* Him."

Ever since my friend's wisdom filled my heart, I have chosen to see my life as a canvas that I'm painting *with* God. He, the Great Artist, is partnering with me to *create* an unfolding work of beauty in my life.

He's doing the same in yours, too.

Our lives are in the hands of the Great Artist. He never makes mistakes. He never questions the art He's creating. He creates in partnership with us. He doesn't force us or manipulate us. He loves us and wants to use His brush strokes to splash life and color onto our dull surfaces. He wants to build texture, layer, and depth. He thrills in taking the blank canvas of our lives, that which we see as the "unknown," and morphing it into beauty and adventure.

And at the end of the day, we may not know exactly how the painting will evolve, what the final piece might look like, or where it will end up. We are certain of one thing, though. We know the Artist, and we know that He makes all things good and beautiful in His time and His way.

So, just paint, friends. Don't stop. Just paint.

*During my years at Hillsong, God whispered to me that painting was going to be part of my tent-making. To view or purchase my artwork, please visit: www.etsy.com/nz/shop/GloryBCreative.

WHEREVER... We'll Go

Post-Ramblings

"Then I heard the voice of the Lord saying, 'Whom shall I send? And who will go for us?' And I said, 'Here am I. Send me!'" ~ Isaiah 6:8 (NIV)

As I think about you reading these stories, my heart is pumping and thumping. Passion is pounding at the door of my heart. It is itching to break through the solid structure of an antiquated wooden door, to smash through completely, splintering the wood into tiny fragments.

This passion is to see a generation – *your* generation – that loves authentically and wholly, a generation that fights for what is right, choosing its battles with wisdom and discernment. I see a people clamoring forward to step into what is good and beautiful, forgetting the visually aesthetic and glitz of fortune and power – those things that appeal to culture. I see a generation rising out of the ashes of consumerism and self-engrossment, traveling together to see God's fame and glory replace the fame and renown of celebrity status. I see a new wave of people who carry the influence of truth, as empowered by the Holy Spirit.

I've been blessed beyond my wildest imagination to travel the untamed, uncharted roads of God's divine navigation. He has been my tour guide. I have not only seen what my worldly eyes have set out to see, but by God's grace, I have seen glimpses of His mighty power at work along these roads.

God's goodness has pried-open the blinds of culture, pulling them apart with His tender strength, so that I can view things from His vantage point. I want to see as He sees. I want to love as He loves. I want to become as He *is*. My culture will not define me because He *is* my culture.

And at the end of the day, above all else, I want to see a generation that knows this ride, this adventure, these uncharted waters are absolutely, without a doubt, *worth it*.

Wherever You lead, we'll go. Let our stories be for Your glory.

"Here we are, Lord, send us…"
    Amen.

ACKNOWLEDGMENTS

"It takes a village to raise a child." In my case, it's taken many villages all around the world to raise me, and more importantly, *lift* me up.

I'd like to thank those who have believed in my "out-of-the-box" missionary lifestyle from the start. Those who gave me hugs and high-fives in big moments and small ones. I'd like to thank my male pastors who have told me that my voice as a woman is important to the work of the kingdom and put action to their words by giving me opportunities to do what I was created to do. I'm so blessed by "soul friends" (Kerstin, Hannah, Carmen, Linda) that are literally scattered across the globe. You are the "Aaron"s that repeatedly lift my arms in battle. And to the countless families (Bentzens, Luedtkes, O'Connors, Anto Castle and others) that have housed a wandering missionary and made me feel at *home* with you, thank you.

I'm thankful for the creative genius of Mark Fansler for his techy help with my book cover layout. I'm thankful for my editors: Kathy Anderson, Erica Anderson, Rebecca Anderson, Becky Fudge, Hannah Wickins, Kerstin Lambert and for Lacie Hicks, who has given so much of her time to help me publish this life-long dream. I'd also like to thank my BSF group who rallied around me in prayer and support along the way.

I'm grateful to *Blue Fuego* for lighting a fire beneath me to finish this book, and to every friend that kept asking me when it was going to be finished. That question drove me to see this through to the end.

I'm grateful for my Advocacy Team (Brian, Meredith, Genena, Catherine) for sharpening me and pushing me into Bigger God things. And for my Swiss Goat Farm "fr-amily" (Craig, Sharon, Ian, Emily, Kerstin, Kevin) that have helped fan the flame of my faith and for their belief in the soon-coming 8th pair of shoes.

I'm thankful for my family, who loves me just the way I am and sometimes makes fun of my odd pronunciation of words. And for my parents, Jim and Kathy Anderson, who have been key forces of strength and tenacity in my life. They believed in me from the moment they laid eyes on me, and their cheers have carried me through the darkest of nights since then with much joy, laughter, and numerous theatrical renditions of "Happy Birthday." You win the "#1 Parents" award - words will never be enough to thank you for all that you are to me and for all you have done for me.

And lastly, I'm especially humbled and honored that God has given me a blank canvas and asked me to paint this life with Him. Jesus is always with me - He's my favorite travel companion, closest friend, and I will chase after Him for the rest of my life.

These stories are for His glory.

ABOUT THE AUTHOR

J. Bethany Anderson is an artist, worship leader, writer, speaker, and global-citizen, having called France, Switzerland, South Africa, Australia and England home. *Kiss My Fish* is her first book and the culmination of heart palpitations and sleepless nights of never giving up on a dream whittled deep into her soul. She's grateful this book is in your hands and prays you will be lifted by *hope* as you read it.

Bethany currently lives in McKinney, Texas, where she was born and raised, and works as freelance artist and ministry leader with ROYAL Corporation. She has a heart for social justice issues, empowering women, and championing Millennials. She is passionate about prayer, spiritual formation, and life as an adventure with God. Bethany loves speaking in accents, feasting on chips and salsa, and traveling the world as much as possible.

www.jbethanyanderson.com
jbethanyanderson.wordpress.com
www.etsy.com/nz/shop/GloryBCreative
www.WeAreROYAL.com

Made in the USA
Columbia, SC
29 September 2019